MUSINGS FROM AN OLD WOODEN BRIDGE

Biblical wisdom for a world gone mad

MJ GAYLOR

WESTBOW
PRESS®
A DIVISION OF THOMAS NELSON
& ZONDERVAN

WestBow Press books may be ordered through booksellers or by contacting:

WestBow Press
A Division of Thomas Nelson & Zondervan
1663 Liberty Drive
Bloomington, IN 47403
www.westbowpress.com
844-714-3454

ISBN: 978-1-6642-7351-1 (sc)
ISBN: 978-1-6642-7353-5 (hc)
ISBN: 978-1-6642-7352-8 (e)

Library of Congress Control Number: 2022913704

Print information available on the last page.

WestBow Press rev. date: 08/05/2022

"It is an ironic habit of human beings to run faster when they have lost their way."

ROLLO MAY

Contents

bisbeesworld.org

I am filled with gratitude for my chief editor, Karen Gaylor, and her team Susan Jordan and Caleb Bryan. Their tireless work, chewing over every sentence, and grappling with each thought, is, and always will be, greatly appreciated.

I wish to dedicate this book to the congregation of The Church at Sun Coast in Jacksonville, Florida for whom I have had the great joy of leading these past twenty years. I have never known a more musing people in all my journeys. They think deeply, love passionately, and serve endlessly. I look forward to spending eternity with them musing by the River of Life.

Prologue

There was an old wooden bridge spanning the stream that ran behind our house on North Grand. A black walnut tree grew along the trail leading to the bridge, and cows dotted a nearby pasture. A large aspen grew out of the creek, providing shade in the hot summer and limbs strong enough to climb. For hours I would sit on that bridge and dangle my feet above the flowing water. I would watch the water gliders make their way through the gentle currents and look for crayfish peering out from underneath the stones that filled the brook. I can still hear the buzz of the dragonflies as they attempted to lite on the sedge grass. The sound of the passing brook was restful and channeled me into magical moments. Sitting on the sturdy planks of that old wooden bridge, I would daydream until I heard my mother calling.

The busy years have not erased the sheer pleasure of those moments, where time did not matter, and schedules did not pull my attention away from the simplicity of a blue bird resting on a willow branch. That old wooden bridge was a place where I gave my mind permission to wonder and my imagination freedom to roam about the countryside. I had time to ponder life and the world around me. I would think about my friends and family. I reflected on the meaning of life and where it would take me. In a word, I mused.

As I grow older, I find myself longing to return to that place of musing. I want to sit on that old bridge again and stare into the water. Many of the questions of my youth have been answered, but still, I want to remain curious. There are still mountains to climb and rivers to traverse, and so, I want to keep asking the questions that make life worth living. I refuse to waste my remaining days in a rush of frivolous activity. The sacredness of solitude calls out to me, and I want to answer. I never want to lose the magic of musing and the resulting adventures.

It has been said that we never view the same stream twice. The flow of life is constantly changing. The brook flows heavy with the winter thaw and then returns to its gentle meandering in summer only to be filled with fallen leaves as the year wanes. Rocks are polished smooth by the pressure of the current, and creek banks erode to create new eddies. Children grow up and bring back with them little bundles of energy called grandkids. Romances blossom, thrilling the soul, and people die, leaving deep gaping holes in our hearts. The stream incessantly babbles with a different song with each rising sun. I want to continue to grow as life's stream changes over time and current. I want to capture every season in its fullness.

There *is* one difference from those days of my youth on the old wooden bridge. I have met the Master of the stream, and I have found his voice to be the sweetest of all. His daily call for me to walk with him along the banks is irresistible and has become the reason I live. It is my hope that you will hear his voice as you read the following pages.

The book in your hands contains no plan or sequential order. There is no attempt to build an argument that reaches a crescendo with four points and a poem. It is simply a collection of random musings because life is random. One of the beauties of sitting on an old wooden bridge, staring into the water, is that your mind drifts with reckless abandonment. The deepest and best thoughts of life come in this way. So, come muse with me. Let's sit on the old wooden bridge together and stare into life's stream.

CHAPTER 1

Life Cycles

In the classic children's story, *Peter Pan*, J.M. Barrie tells the tale of a boy who refuses to grow up. Peter, having rejected life's march toward maturity, goes to live in Neverland as the leader of the lost boys. On that mystical island, he battles Captain Hook, gains a fairy as a friend, and eventually meets Wendy, Michael, and John Darling. The story has been a favorite for generations and finds its enduring quality in our desire to live forever in the fantasy of our childhood. For boys at least, an island filled with warring Indians and dangerous pirates adds to the draw. However, the time comes when we must all grow up. Eventually, we must all face the rigors of adulthood. The only question that remains is how successful our transition will be to the mainland of maturity. Will we land on happy shores?

One of the secrets of a successful life is our ability to navigate change. Childhood yields to adolescence, and then before our wondering eyes, adulthood emerges. The ugly caterpillar becomes a beautiful butterfly or vice versa. Sociologists call these periods *life cycles*. God has designed this transitional process for our growth and development. Shakespeare, in his play, *As you Like It*, suggested that there are seven stages of a man. The first stage is infancy followed by schoolboy, lover, soldier, justice, and then the apathy of old age. The last stage culminating in an oblation to God. The movie, *The Curious Case of Benjamin Buttons*, is a story about what happens when these life cycles are reversed. Benjamin Buttons was born old and then grew younger with each passing year. It is a sad movie that reminds us that God's design is perfect. Jesus himself went through the growth process as we see him as a twelve-year-old boy in the temple asking and answering the questions of the Scribes. After this moment in the temple, he returned to Nazareth with his mother and Joseph. Furthermore, the Son of man was part of a family of brothers and sisters. Jesus took care of his mother after Joseph died, carrying on the family business. He was a young man growing up in a small town. Through all of this, Jesus transitioned from a child into a man by natural processes. "And Jesus increased in wisdom and in stature and in favor with God and man."[1]

Successfully transitioning from one stage of life to the next requires something psychologists call *closure*. Closure is the moment we stand at the entrance to a new phase of our lives and turn to wave goodbye to who we were in the past. The lover, having fallen in love, bids the schoolboy goodbye and, in a few years, goes off to fight the battles of life as a soldier. One cycle must end before the next one can begin. As we grow, our former lifecycle dies giving birth to new responsibilities and hopefully better decision making. The apostle Paul stated, "When I was a child, I spoke like a child, I thought like a child, I reasoned like a child. When I became a man, I gave up childish ways."[2] Paul's statement of healthy growth and transition is encapsulated by his last few words, "I gave up childish things."[3] Maturity from adolescence to adulthood brings with it a recognition that certain behavior and pursuits are self-centered.

If our time in any life cycle has been satisfying and fulfilling, then our passage to the next becomes easier. It is possible to become stuck in a life cycle when our experience during that time has been difficult. Psychologists call this *unfinished business*. Unresolved life experiences can haunt us for the rest our lives, and this is where the trouble begins. We either refuse or are unable to move on into the next phase of life successfully. For whatever reason, tragedy, unfulfilled needs, or not being challenged by others, we remain where we are in life. Examples are sadly too numerous to mention, but here are a few. There are many forty-year-olds still living in the basement of their parent's home, acting like they are thirteen. Some elderly folks are still battling with their siblings over who got Grandma's tea set. Unfortunately, this can also happen to us spiritually. For various reasons, a believer can become stunted in their growth to the point where they remain immature. Let us examine the process.

When a person becomes a Christian, the Bible describes them as a babe in Christ. This is all quite natural, and the Scripture does not condemn the expression. Paul describes this phase of immaturity when he stated, "But I, brothers, could not address you as spiritual people, but as people of the flesh, as infants in Christ."[4]

They were described as "people of the flesh" because they were still relying on their own strength to live out the Christian life. They were not being overtly sinful; they were simply relying on an inadequate source to live godly. This self-reliance is the characteristic of a new believer, for this is all they know. Looking to our own strength to walk with God is a phase that marks the babe in Christ, not those who are reaching full age. Complete reliance on Christ is the place of victory for healthy, growing believers. Paul's rebuke involved the fact that they should have been eating meat and were still on a milky diet. They were not moving on in their spiritual lives as evident in their divisive spirit. The difference between a babe in Christ and a mature believer is a matter of origin and source. The former relies on self and the latter on Christ alone.

The main characteristic of immaturity is self-centeredness. A child naturally thinks the world revolves around them and their needs. A babe in Christ believes that God exists to meet their needs. They believe that the gospel is primarily about them and their need of salvation. Maturity is evident when a believer begins to understand that the gospel is about Christ and the glory of God. Salvation may have been the result of faith, but it is not its final expression. According to Paul, the ultimate issuance of our redemption is that Christ might be seen in us.[5] This alone brings glory to God when he sees his Son manifested through our lives.

When I was new in the faith, God gave me the opportunity to meet some amazing believers. They were older men who had walked with Christ many years. I saw in their lives, and especially in their eyes, something I desired. They possessed a quiet strength, that only Christ can give. I wanted to walk in that same path. I desired others to see Christ in me with the same richness of spirit that I was privileged to witness in those men. This alone is what brings glory to God. Therefore, even though it takes time and there are many obstacles, it is vitally important that we grow strong in faith. Our maturation is not only a blessing to our souls, but more importantly, it is the way that God uses us to further his kingdom and bring glory to his name.

When the apostle Paul wrote to the Romans, he was writing to a church he had never visited. In his opening remarks, he stated his desire to come to them, to impart some *spiritual gift*. He also desired to receive some "spiritual gift" from them.[6] He never identified what the gift was, which fills me with questions. What gift of his was he referring to? Having never met them, how did he know what spiritual gift they had to offer?

Since Paul was writing to his brothers in Christ, we know that they had already received the Holy Spirit. Further, we know that spiritual gifts are given by God, not man, and so, these cannot be in view. Paul's gift to them was the expression of Christ, as seen through his unique personality. Their gift to him was Jesus living out his life through them. It was their mutual faith as displayed in their human individuality.

When his life begins to grow in us, something amazing occurs. He takes our unique personality and causes it to find its fulfillment in Christ. In other words, an individual that has never existed before begins to emerge. It is called, *Christ in me*. We are all new creatures in Christ.[7] All of us have something to share with our fellow believers that is so distinctive and matchless, that no one else can duplicate our ministry. Our lives, in Christ, are like wood that the master craftsman has spent time carving. Jesus brings out the beauty from the hidden grains of our God-given personality. God has given us closure to our past life, so we transition by faith into a life that pleases him. There is no unfinished business once we see ourselves in Christ alone.

We all look beautifully different in Christ, and this is the *gift* we need from one another. Therefore, fellowship with others is vital. The importance of being involved in the lives of fellow Christians cannot be overstated. We all need to be a vital part of the church we attend. Take your gift, *Christ in you* and mix it up with *Christ in them*. God is creating vessels of honor, and the gift we give one another is a beautiful and precious experience that changes and alters what it touches. It may take many years to fully develop, but when his life is seen in us, we become a gift to all those we meet. *Christ in us*, becomes a gift to be opened and enjoyed by countless others throughout our lifetime.

For everything there is a season, and a time for every matter under heaven.

ECCLESIASTES 3:1 ESV

CHAPTER 2

Generation Redeemed

At the beginning of the last century, for some unknown reason, we began to name our generations. Evidently, we had more time on our hands than our ancestors. At any rate, it began with *The Greatest Generation* who arrived in the early 1900s. They earned that title by rebuilding America after the Great Depression and then defeating the Nazis in World War II. *The Silent Generation* came along in the mid 1920s and were so named because the children of that era were told to be seen and not heard. They gave us jazz, swing dancing, great movies, and a little rodent named Mickey Mouse. When soldiers returned from World War II, they celebrated by giving us hordes of newborns called the "baby boomers." This generation was known for peace rallies, rejecting authority, getting high on LSD, and living with a newfound sense of freedom from old norms. Marches on Washington were a common sight at that time. *Generation X* began showing up in the mid 60s and were defined by a desire to achieve all their parents had in a very short period. This resulted in a generation deeply in debt and profoundly unhappy. Beginning in the early 80s the millennials arrived on the scene and are best known for being *The Peter Pan Generation*. So called because they simply did not want to grow up. Some of them are still living in their parent's basement to this day. Finally, *The Z Generation* began to grace our planet in the mid

90s. Deeply dependent on technology, they have never known a world without the internet or a smart phone. They turn the pages of a book with a swipe, rather than the lick of a finger. For them, information is only a Google search away.

However, there is another generation I would like us to consider that has been largely ignored by the world. Unlike all the other layers of humanity, this generation can pinpoint the day they arrived. It was early on a Sunday morning 2000 years ago. The event included an earthquake, descending angels, an empty tomb, and a man who came back from the dead. Guarding his gravesite were two Roman soldiers who fell as dead men when angels appeared. Apparently, the arrival of the angels was too much for the two battle-hardened soldiers. In contrast, when three Jewish women approached the tomb, they did what the soldiers could not do. They remained on their feet when they saw the angels. The women carefully listened to the angel's announcement and then ran to tell the men in their company what they had seen. These men, who were hiding in fear of their lives, promptly refused to believe the women's report.[8] They remained in unbelief until they had seen for themselves that their leader had indeed come back from the dead.

The resurrection of that man created a regeneration of people who have endured to this day. They are called, *Generation Redeemed*, and they have a story to tell that is unlike any other. The authorities immediately attempted to suppress this generation by saying that the body of the man who came out of the tomb had been stolen. However, their evil plan fell woefully short when he appeared to more than five hundred of his followers at one time. Fifty days later his disciples were huddled together in an upper room when a mighty rushing wind filled the chamber. Tongues of fire rested upon each of them, giving them the ability and boldness to proclaim the resurrection of their leader. Coming out of hiding and spilling onto the porch of the upper room, this tiny group faced thousands with an offer to join them and march toward a kingdom that was not of this world.

The authorities in that day worked hard to extinguish the fire of this new people group but to no avail. The wind gusts of their hatred and persecution only served to fan the flame and intensify the fire of this new generation. In fact, the efforts of governments throughout the ages to destroy *Generation Redeemed* have only helped to fuel its growth. This subset of society belongs to a new creation and even though they live among the other generations, they are not a part of them. Now, for the best news of all, *Generation Redeemed* is not a cliquish, exclusive people group that is impossible to join. All are welcome to become a part of *Generation Redeemed* but only on one condition. To join a person must believe in the One who died for them and then came out of that tomb. They must renounce all other allegiances and cling only to him. There was a Jewish Pharisee in the first century that had to learn this truth.

Nicodemus was an old religious man who had seen it all, but he had never met anyone like Jesus Christ. He was so impressed with this young rabbi that he orchestrated a nighttime rendezvous to probe his mind and discover his secrets. Imagine his surprise when Jesus insisted that he needed spiritual life before he could understand anything about God. He needed to be born again. To Nicodemus, his entire religious experience could be summed up in four words… "How can a man…?" Jesus answered that a man can do nothing to earn Heaven. To be born a second time was the work of God alone. "No one has ascended into Heaven except he who descended from Heaven, the Son of Man."[9] Nicodemus could not make it to Heaven by his own good works. No man can enter the heavenly gates without the miracle of the spiritual birth.

As the wind blew through their hair that night, Jesus looked up and smiled. After seeing the watery eyes of Nicodemus, Jesus told him the way of the Spirit was like the breeze. You can't see the wind or dictate its movements, but nevertheless you know it's real. Becoming a part of *Generation Redeemed* requires a transformation within, which defies tangible evidence but first and foremost provides unspeakable reality. Through faith in Christ, a man's life is changed into what the Bible calls a new creation. To join *Generation Redeemed*, a person must bend their knee and give their heart to Jesus Christ. All the work has already been accomplished to achieve this transformation. All that is required is to believe. A new family bloodline is available to whosoever will come. All are welcomed at the foot of the cross. Generations come and go, but those who belong to *Generation Redeemed* are awaiting the return of Jesus and the glories of Heaven. They will spend all eternity together as fellow worshippers of the one true God.

༺◌ༀ◌༻

And you have made them a kingdom and praise to our God, and they shall reign on earth.

REVELATION 5:10 ESV

CHAPTER 3

Vanity

L ast week I pushed a tree down with my bare hands. In the event you are not yet impressed with this herculean feat, the monster before me stood thirty foot high, and its base was bigger than I could put my arms around. With a shout and a shove, it came down with a thud. As Goliath stood before David, the old timber never stood a chance. After beating my chest and howling at the daytime moon, I looked around to see who was watching and discovered it was only my dog, Cooper, running for cover. My chest fell as a deafening silence filled the air. No applause, no victor's crown, no reporters to write of my amazing deed. Not even Paul Bunyan showed up to offer his congratulations. The only thing I saw was a never-ending horde of carpenter ants pouring out from the stomp of the old fallen tree giant. From Goliath's severed head, an army of insect warriors marched to another tree, unimpressed by my moment of glory.

A further analysis of my hollow victory suggested a realization that I had simply pushed over a rotten tree that the wind would have eventually taken down in due course. It dawned on me, standing along the tree line of my property, that most of our efforts as human beings fall in the category of the generally unimpressive. When compared with the feats of the God who made the tree, the strength needed to push it down was laughable. And yet, there I stood waiting for some sort of recognition. At the least I could have been crowned King of the Forest for a day. Other than the admiration on my dog's face, the heavens were silent, and I walked back to my house to lick my bruised ego. In the words parodying Carly Simon, "you're so vain, I bet you think this article is about you."

The Psalmist cried out to ancient Israel, "Surely all mankind stands as a mere breath, surely a man goes about as a shadow."[10] The King James Version renders that verse in the following way, "Surely every man walks in a vain show." Guilty as charged. We walk, we talk, and at the end of the day it is all an empty display of vanity. We puff ourselves up as if we were the next big show on the stage of life, but few, if any, are impressed with our show-stopping performances. If we receive any applause, it is normally from our moms or a kind aunt. When the curtain falls, everyone asks, "Who was that masked man?" Narcissism is a cruel taskmaster. There is little hope in our personal battle against vanity because we are its fountain.

Sampson was one of the last judges in Israel, and his name meant, *Man of the Sun*. He is remembered for his strength and his tumultuous relationship with Delilah, but there is so much more to learn. Long before Sampson was born, his mother received a prophecy from the Angel of the Lord that he would deliver his people from the Philistines. No doubt, this story was told to Sampson as a young boy. His young mind became imprinted with the image of his own importance.

In the course of time, Samson grew to be physically impressive with long, flowing hair. When he came of age to marry, he approached his parents. "Then he came up and told his father and mother, "I saw one of the daughters of the Philistines at Timnah. Now get her for me as my wife."[11] Notice the tone in his demand, *get her for me*. They objected because the woman was not Jewish, and Samson doubled down. "But Samson said to his father, 'Get her for me, for she is right in my eyes.'"[12] There was a lack of respect in his voice as he demanded what pleased his eyes. This ultimatum of Samson reveals a serious character flaw that was present long before the advent of his dating life. Obviously, this was a young man who had never been told no nor denied anything he wanted. He was accustomed to getting his way.

If you want to create a young man or woman who is filled with vanity, then give them everything they want from the time they are a child. Succumb to their every whim and when they attempt to manipulate you, capitulate to their every demand. I suspect that the parents of Samson were intimidated by this young boy, having received such an incredible prophecy concerning him. They made the common mistake of valuing the gift of God more than God himself. They refused to do the hard work of disciplining their son as a child and suffered the consequences of a rebellious young man.

When Delilah's father denied Sampson's request, he flew into a rage. Apparently, his temper was hot and had never been restrained. He simply would not be denied the craving of his eyes. In the end, he was easily betrayed by Delilah. His vanity was his downfall.

Unfortunately, Sampson was driven by his uncontrollable passions because he had never been trained to deny them. Narcissism became a beast that eventually cost him his eyes and his life. Even the wicked Philistines became weary of his roaming eyes. The man, whose entire life was a show of arrogance and pride, brought the house down when he committed suicide. Samson's showstopping moment between the pillars was a tragic ending to a life filled with vanity and unrestrained passions. The *Man of the Sun* lived a very dark life in the shadow of his own pretentious vanity.

I am convinced we all take ourselves much too seriously. We all share the unfortunate propensity to place our eyes on our own achievements and talents, and as a result, become too impressed with ourselves. In effect, we waste too much time riding on our own parade float, waiting for the adoring masses to recognize our ordinary accomplishments. So, what is the answer to our dilemma? It is to be conquered by One greater than ourselves. Victory over vanity is achieved when we understand that the true hero in life is Jesus Christ. He alone deserves glory and praise, and we are but vessels in his hand. If we accomplish anything of merit, it is because he has first worked within us that victory. Jesus is the cause, and we are the effect. When we understand this truth, the pressure to perform and please whoever we think needs pleasing is gone. The weight of life evaporates like a puff of smoke. Jesus said, "Without me you can do nothing."[13]

Solomon wrote, "Vanity of vanities, says the Preacher, vanity of vanities! All is vanity."[14] All of life is an empty performance without God. The only truly impressive thing in life is what God has done through his blessed Son to bring about the salvation of all mankind. When Jesus died on the cross, he pushed over the monster oak of sin with one hand. He then cut it at the root and set fire to it. Soon, it will be nothing but a pile of potash. The army of carpenter ants that tunnel and destroy are gone. He cancelled the penalty of sin in its fall, broke the power of sin when he cut its roots, and he will soon cause sin to flee our very presence forever. Rather than the rotten trees we push over in life, God should be our constant preoccupation and glory. His victory over sin provides for us the victor's crown. So, quit the show, walk out the stage door and into the blessed sunlight of self-forgetfulness. Jesus is the main attraction.

⊙〰〰⊙

Surely every man walketh in a vain show: surely, they are disquieted in vain: he heapeth up riches, and knoweth not who shall gather them.

PSALMS 39:6 KJV

CHAPTER 4

The Impossible Made Easy

Honus Wagner was too small to play professional baseball. To make matters worse he was bowlegged. However, defying critics and sportswriters alike, he became one of the greatest shortstops to ever play the game. By the time the *Flying Dutchman* retired in 1917, he had set enough batting and fielding records to become one of the original inductees into the Hall of Fame in Cooperstown, New York. When asked about his amazing journey and his ability to overcome the odds, he famously replied, "There ain't much to being a ballplayer if you're a ballplayer."[15] In other words, if playing the game is in you, then everything else comes with practice. At the core of Honus Wagner there was a ballplayer dying to get out.

This is true of all of us. We have all been given gifts and talents by our Creator. The drives and passions within excite our interests, and if given enough attention, these intrinsic ambitions become reality. Life is organic in nature, and thus, operates on this principle. The seed determines the ultimate expression of the plant as it grows. Now, what is true in the natural world finds its equal manifestation in the realm of the spiritual world. Humanity, born from the seed of Adam, will display a sinful nature until a different seed is planted that changes this dynamic. That seed is the life of Christ planted in us at the moment of the new birth.

In its simplest definition, the Christian life is the outflowing expression of Christ's life in us. There are many doctrines to learn, but this singular truth is the starting place for growth in the spiritual life. The Bible declares that Christ dwells in the life of the believer.[16] In the same way that blood courses through our veins, he channels his life through us. This life-giving source is as sure as the evening tide and as faithful as the rising sun. Irrespective of what we see in the mirror each morning, or how our mood swings, we know that his life abides within. We rest on this unchanging truth regardless of our experience of it.

Throughout Galatia, the apostle Paul agonized to see Jesus expressing himself through the believers. He wrote, "My little children, for whom I am again in the anguish of childbirth until Christ is formed in you!"[17] Progress is accomplished organically, not with the machinery of effort, and that is the key. Growth is the essential need and faith is the wheel that turns the turbine. In the case of Honus Wagner, he was born to play baseball. Likewise, in the case of the believer, we are reborn to express God's nature, and again, this is accomplished in a very intrinsic, organic way. Consider again nature as an illustration. The seed of every living thing contains the entire blueprint of the plant or tree. All it needs is to be planted in the soil and given the right conditions for its growth and expression. Nature takes its course regardless of our fretting and hand wringing.

Jesus said, "Abide in me, and I in you. As the branch cannot bear fruit by itself, unless it abides in the vine, neither can you, unless you abide in me."[18] Our great need is to rest and trust the work of God, not a *pull yourself up by the boot-straps* mentality. Peter stated, "According to his divine power he has given us all things that pertain to life and godliness, through the knowledge of him that has called us to knowledge and virtue."[19]

As a result of our Christian growth, the outward manifestation of Jesus Christ is revealed. This expression is simply an outgrowth of the inward reality of the Holy Spirit. To borrow from Wagner's home-spun observation, "There ain't much to being a Christian, if you're a Christian." To some this sounds simplistic. However, the very best things in life are simple and God has not made the Christian life difficult. In fact, he has made it impossible. We fail because we exert effort. All the work has been placed on Christ. We abide in his resurrected life, and he supplies all that we need for growth. This is the great truth to be learned. Years ago, we had a dear Japanese lady who attended our church whose name was Tosiko Bower. Occasionally, I would call from the pulpit and ask her to *try* to be Japanese. Her response was always the same, "I don't have to *try* to be Japanese, I *am* Japanese."

Nowhere is this truth seen with more clarity than in the Sermon on the Mount. In the opening eight Beatitudes, Jesus reveals the character of those who inhabit his kingdom. In this sermon, he does not direct his followers to do anything; he declares who they already are because of being his disciples. Blessed *are* the poor, the meek, those who mourn, etc. Jesus did not say blessed are those who do these things; he said blessed *are* the merciful, peacemakers, and so on. By focusing on Christ's life within, the Christian expresses the tenants of the Sermon on the Mount naturally. Our lives reflect his true nature, revealing that we are citizens of the kingdom of God. We don't start by doing anything; we begin by believing that we fully possess his life, and that life emulates the character traits described in the Beatitudes. The Christian life is a beautiful impossibility, and failure helps us to understand this truth.

Peter denied his Lord three times. Thomas doubted the resurrection until he thrust his hand in the side of Jesus. James and John had to be rebuked for their condemning spirit toward the Samaritans. Martha found fault with her sister Mary for worshiping at the feet of the Master. On the eve of the crucifixion, the apostles got into an argument about who would be the greatest. Failure after failure accentuates our desperate need of him. We only look up when we are flat on our back. We must come to realize that apart from him we will always fall short.

Apart from him we utterly fail the King's edicts because the Sermon on the Mount was never meant for us. The Beatitudes were meant for the life he would place in us after we are born again. If Jesus is a teacher only, then he has set us up for failure, but if he is a Savior, then he has given us an ideal that only he can realize after we are saved. A teacher gives us knowledge in the hope that we will allow it to guide our lives. There is no intrinsic motivation or power given by our instructors. A Savior gives us deliverance from the dilemma of our depravity and fills us to live out his teachings. Jesus does not help us be meek; he is the meekness in us that he requires of us. This is all activated by faith. I no longer trust myself to be pure in heart; he *is* my purity. I no longer look to myself to be a peacemaker; he is the peacemaker in me. Augustine once prayed, "Lord, whatever you require of me, first accomplish in me."[20] You see, there's not a lot to being a Christian, if you are one.

꿍뀪

Blessed are the pure in heart, for they shall see God.

MATTHEW 5:8 ESV

CHAPTER 5

Reclaimed Lives

One man's junk is another man's treasure. This well-worn expression finds its ultimate fulfillment in pawnshops and garage sales. Within these second-hand strip stores, items fill the shelves longing to be taken home and be made useful again. Hand-written prices are tagged on each item expressing the shop owners estimate of their value. Refurnished, recovered, or reclaimed, the stuff that once cluttered an old machine shed, is now proudly on display.

Recently, a neighbor allowed me to dig in an old, dilapidated barn on her property to reclaim the wood. After a long process of restoration, the old slats came to life, and the finished product was a thing to behold. My friend's barn was a literal gold mine sitting in the woods, waiting for some prospector with a hammer and a crowbar to mine its beauty. In the world of wood working there is nothing more valuable than reclaimed wood. Whether it's an old broke-down barn or an item found in a pawnshop, a keen eye wins the day.

Reclaiming old barns is a recent phenomenon; however, turning discarded junk into something valuable is nothing new in the spiritual world. God has been rummaging through the junkyards of this world for thousands of years to find men and women to serve and love him. Paul reminded the church at Corinth that the world was filled with thieves, idolaters, and sexual deviants. He then declared, "and such were some of you."²¹ Those redeemed folks in Corinth had been embroiled in the same sinful lifestyles as the pagan world. The difference between those inside the church and those in the world was the restoration process of God's grace. He had reclaimed them. He had so fully recovered them by his blood that they were washed clean, sanctified, and justified in Christ Jesus. The same is true of everyone who knows Christ. This was also true for the thief who died next to Jesus.

Regarding this thief, we know little of the man who hung on the cross next to Jesus other than he began his day in a dingy prison cell and ended it in Paradise. The records show that he was a thief and for that crime he was sentenced to death. Now, crucifixion seems like a harsh penalty for stealing something, but regardless, that was his fate. Perhaps, he was a repeat offender, and the patience of the Romans had grown thin. Was he sorry for the choices he had made? Did he regret a life of crime, or had it been only a single incident that landed him in prison? We simply don't know. What we do know is that he was facing a cruel death. A wooden cross, three nails, and a saddle, were the instruments of death. After days, or sometimes even weeks, a man would die of either exposure or suffocation. The thief was facing a merciless death. He would experience horrendous torture as he stepped out of the prison that day. Strange as it may sound, though, he was exactly where God wanted him to be. Something unexpectedly happened to this man that day on Golgotha's Hill.

Having been led outside the walls of Jerusalem with two other men, he watched as a crowd gathered. What could possibly be the attraction, he thought? It angered him to think people had nothing better to do than watch him die in such a way. Lying down on the splintered beam he looked up into the clouds and wondered if the next life would bring him a better lot. He hoped it would be better than the miserable years he had spent on earth. The iron peg was cold against his skin. The sound of the hammer pierced his eardrum as he felt the violence of its sharpened point driving through flesh and bone. The cross was lifted high and dropped into place. There was nothing left for him to do but look into the empty faces in the crowd and wait for death. But the crowd wasn't looking back at him. All eyes were on the figure next to him, the man in the middle. He saw an older woman softly crying next to a young man before that center cross. Looking to his left, the thief saw two Pharisees with sorrow in their eyes. In the gathering were temple guards, foreigners, and the women who always came to comfort the criminals with gall. Robed men from the Sanhedrin walked back and forth wagging their fingers at the man in the middle. A wicked look of satisfaction spread across their faces like wild animals that had cornered their prey.

And then there was the man opposite from him snarling and spitting venom at the man in the middle. The stranger next to him remained quiet with a look of determination on his face. His entire body appeared like raw meat from a butcher shop. It won't take long for him to die, he thought. The thief joined in with slanderous insults of his own, directed at the man in the middle. Suddenly, lightning flashed as thunder pounded the hillside. The thief turned his head and looked into the eyes of the stranger. The man was looking at him with compassion. His eyes, caked with dried blood, were filled with love. The thief quickly looked away, shame filling his soul. He knew he deserved to be there, but not this man.

The shouting on the ground gradually faded into mere chatter. The man opposite him continued to spew insults, but the thief heard only his heart beating wildly in his chest. The sign above him said that he was a king. Who was this stranger? Even though he was covered with blood, he looked majestic. Did he dare ask the question that was on his lips? Then, in barely a whisper, the thief, who had caused so much pain and wasted his life, asked to be remembered when this stranger came into his kingdom. "Truly," the man in the middle said, "today you will be with me in paradise."[22]

Time ground to a sudden halt. He could not describe it, but somehow, he had been set free. All the evil he had ever done no longer mattered. All the wasted years were forgotten in the anticipation of a glorious future. He had never, before that day, met the man in the middle, but he knew before the sun went down, he would walk with him for all eternity. The suffering continued, but he could now endure its pain knowing it would not last forever. The cursing crowd stayed until the bitter end, but they had no effect on him. His soul was finally at peace. He could do nothing to repay the man in the middle, but it did not matter. His life had been reclaimed in his last few waning moments. He had become a priceless treasure to Jesus Christ.

A while back I purchased a hall tree cabinet made of reclaimed wood. As I read the information from the manufacturer, I thought about our lives as believers. On the back of the hall tree was a note that read, *The beauty of reclaimed wood is in its imperfections.* I smiled. It was the knots, cracks and damaged areas that added character to each piece, giving the furniture a distinct personality all its own. The same is true of us. Real mashed potatoes have lumps. A mark on the arm of a chair adds to the character of the piece. The digs and scars in the wood flooring tell the stories of the people who lived there. No cover up is necessary.

We tend to cover the damaged areas of our lives from others when it is those very imperfections that others need to see. God doesn't cover the hammer marks or look away from the ugly knots of our former lives or our present mistakes. The beauty in our lives is not the projecting of a perfect life but in bringing glory to a God who recovers the sinner from the rusty machine sheds of life. Jesus doesn't hide the place that's been damaged; he allows his grace to make it beautiful. He brings beauty out of ashes.[23] Only Jesus can salvage the wood from the dilapidated barns of this world. What men throw away, God recovers and reclaims for his own. Heaven alone will tell the stories of God's trophies of grace. Perhaps, this is why we will throw our crowns at his feet.

⌘

And such were some of you. But you were washed, you were sanctified, you were justified in the name of the Lord Jesus Christ and by the Spirit of our God.

1 CORINTHIANS 6:11 ESV

CHAPTER 6

Loved by God

Ann Landers once wrote, "Love is friendship that has caught fire. It is quiet understanding, mutual confidence, sharing and forgiving. It is loyalty through good and bad times. It settles for less than perfection and makes allowances for human weaknesses."[24] Good quote. Landers captures the elusive topic of love with some practical insights into its true expression. True love begins with friendship and then grows into an inexhaustible fire. It finds its ultimate fulfillment despite human frailty through understanding and forgiveness.

Ms. Landers certainly encapsulated the ideal, but let's be real, that kind of love is hard to pull off. Settling for less than perfect and making allowances for human weakness sounds good but dealing with imperfect people sometimes gets under our skin. We want our friends and family to at least measure up to some standard of acceptable behavior, and we feel quite comfortable to set the bar. Love also needs to be a two-way street. If we exhaust ourselves meeting people's needs while ours are ignored, well, that tire will go flat quickly. We all struggle with this thing called love. Whether it's between friends or lovers, it tests our resolve to just stay in the game. Love may be the best of things, but it is an elusive treasure at best.

Recently, Karen and I enjoyed the newest installment of *Beauty and the Beast*. It is the mark of great stories that even though we know the ending, we can't get enough of the storyline. Later, I asked my family what lesson could be drawn from this adventurous love story. My daughter-in-law replied, "If you must be kidnaped by a Beast, make sure he's got a great library." I think G.K. Chesterton got a little closer. He wrote, "There is the great lesson of 'Beauty and the Beast'; that a thing must be loved before it is loveable."[25] A true axiom, but it presents a huge problem. There is no love in this world that can truly meet the need of the human heart. Unconditional love is not something people are able to give to one another. Our love is finite, and so, it must always have strings attached to it. As beautiful as human love may seem, it is not sufficient. Meaningful relationships must be fueled from a higher source. We must seek this kind of love from a source outside of ourselves and apart from what another person can give us. We must receive it from God.

When the apostle John told his readers to love one another, he began by reminding them of something vital. He calls them the "Beloved."[26] They were already defined with that enduring term. John reminded them that they were so loved by the Father, that "Beloved" had become their name. This love from God was a gift freely given without any strings attached and separate from merit on the part of the beneficiary. God considered these people his own by virtue of his redemptive work in their lives. According to John, embracing the truth of our relationship with God is the beginning place in our striving to love ourselves and others. There is, though, something else to be considered. Just the knowledge that we are loved by God doesn't necessarily translate into receiving that love in its fulness.

A Pharisee named Simon invited Jesus to dinner. In a country of millions, there were only a few thousand Pharisees, so this invitation was a big deal. The dinner was going well until a woman entered and quietly went straight to Jesus. The religious men and dignitaries in Simon's house recognized the woman as a sinner and were repulsed by her presence. Ignoring the faces that attempted to bring her shame, she fell before Jesus and began to weep and kiss his feet. Her tears ran down his toes, and so, she took her long hair and began to dry them. The awkwardness of the dinner party reached a crescendo when she took a jar filled with alabaster and broke it, pouring it out on Jesus. No one knew what to do except Jesus. He turned to Simon and asked him a question by telling him a story. "A certain moneylender had two debtors. One owed five hundred denarii, and the other fifty. When they could not pay, he cancelled the debt of both. Now which of them will love him more?"[27] It was a rhetorical question and Simon had no choice but to give the obvious answer. "Simon answered, "The one, I suppose, for whom he cancelled the larger debt."[28]

After mumbling his response to Jesus, the Master turned and looked at the woman while still speaking to Simon. "Do you *see* this woman, Simon," he asked.[29] Up to that point, it is unlikely that anyone in the room had really seen her. In their eyes, she was an annoying distraction, an embarrassing situation that needed to be remedied. They saw a woman who did not deserve to be in the same room as they were. These pious Jews were repulsed by this sinful woman, and they wanted her to leave.

Jesus blew right past her sinful history and received the love she was bringing to him. Her actions were a response to the beauty of the Savior and her sin debt being forgiven. We have no record of any interaction between Jesus and this woman. Perhaps, it was simply a look he had given her as he passed through the crowds. Regardless, she got the message and refused to allow anyone to stop her from displaying her love. This woman gained the ability to love through the knowledge of the love Jesus had shown her. She was the only one in the room who was free.

In the eyes of God, we are all equally sinners. Everyone in that room, including Simon the Pharisee, was as sinful as that woman who wept at Jesus's feet. They just refused to admit it. Simon did none of the things that a good host should do because he saw himself as righteous. He could not love because he refused to acknowledge his sin and his need of forgiveness. He could not love because he refused to be loved.

To know that we are loved by God is to understand the sin debt he has canceled for all of us by his death on the cross. The heart of the Father was openly displayed for all to see in that moment of time. True love is not sentimental in nature, neither does it come with strings attached. The love of God, in its most rugged expression, is in the giving of his Son.[30] It is best understood by God's sovereign choice to place his love upon us unconditionally. None of us can merit the love of God, neither can we repay what he has done for us. We honor him most by receiving that love and then walking as the "Beloved."

When we view ourselves as being loved by God, we begin to love ourselves. This is the first step in loving others. When we are convinced that God loves everyone we meet, then they become loveable in our eyes. If we wait for others to attain some standard of loveliness, then we will never love as we should. The greatest love we share as human beings is the love we first receive from God. Just as God gives us his love as a gift, our love to others must likewise be freely given because he first loved us. The Greeks had a word for this kind of love. They called it *agape*, and it is this tenderness that makes human relationships deep and meaningful. The love between friends and lovers alike finds its truest expression as we rest in God's love for us.

ᏩᎳᎧᏇ

Beloved, let us love one another, for
love is from God, and whoever loves has
been born of God and knows God.

I JOHN 4:7 ESV

CHAPTER 7

Coddiwomple

I n 1977, I stepped aboard the USS Patterson in Philadelphia for my first duty. I had chosen that port for reasons that soon fizzled and was left disappointed in my choice of duty. Having joined the Navy to see the world, the last place I wanted to be was in the city of brotherly love. I desperately wanted to be anywhere but Philadelphia. Walking up the gangplank I was greeted with this announcement, "Welcome to the Patterson, we sail for Mayport next week." I was stunned. I had no idea where Mayport was, but neither did I care. Life's currents were in full force, and I was happy to hoist the sail. My life changed dramatically at that moment in ways I could have never imagined and coddiwomple was the best way to describe the experience.

Coddiwomple is an English slang word from the 17th century which means to, *travel purposely toward an as-yet-unknown destination.*[31] Sounds like a good description of life. None of us know where life will ultimately lead, and yet, we nevertheless continue our journey with our ears pinned back and our noses to the grindstone. The word coddiwomple encompasses an even deeper meaning when we apply it to our spiritual journey here on earth. The twists and turns of our earthly pilgrimage have a heavenly purpose and meaning. God is writing our story. Even though we know that Heaven will be our destination, what happens until we arrive is a mystery to us. Our path is fully known by God; to us it is a story yet to be told.

The trail ahead is unmarked, so, pick a direction, and start walking. The unwritten chapters of our lives are only discovered as we travel purposely toward an as-yet-unknown destination. This is the beauty of coddiwomple.

At first glance, coddiwomple appears to be a reckless way to live. Structured people begin to twitch with the thought of living without clear outcomes. "You must have goals, objectives. If you aim at nothing you will hit it every time," they argue. It seemed Abraham was a wandering soul until God called him to leave Ur of the Chaldees. He was given a direction without a destination. "By faith Abraham obeyed when he was called to go out to a place that he was to receive as an inheritance. And he went out, not knowing where he was going."[32]

In his book, *The Seven Habits of Highly Effective People*, Stephen Covey encourages his readers to begin with the end in mind.[33] Covey insists we must know our destination before beginning our journey. In Covey's writings every move should be calculated to bring us to the place in life we desire. Coddiwomple challenges the assumption that we can manipulate our own ends. It suggests the possibility that there are factors beyond our control, unseen forces that will send our tiny boats over a waterfall or onto new waters.

Admittedly, to pack our bags and head out the door without a solid plan in hand appears to be a journey for buffoons. Trusting in providence to snap the pieces of our daily puzzle together may leave us a little unhinged, but the desire to *map out* life kills the adventurer in all of us. Coddiwomple causes the blood to stir and the pulse to quicken. It is exciting to launch out on a new adventure, to explore regions beyond our understanding. In the words of the fictional character, Captain James Kirk, "To boldly go where no man has gone before." Oswald Chambers wrote concerning the graciousness of the unknown, "We are apt to look upon uncertainty as a bad thing, because we are all too mathematical and common sense. We imagine we have to reach an end; so, we have, but a particular end is easily reached, and is not of the nature of spiritual life. The nature of spiritual life is that we are certain in our uncertainty, consequently we do not make our 'nests' anywhere spiritually. Immediately we make a "nest" out of an organization or a creed or a belief, we come across the biggest of calamities, the fact that all certainty brings death."[34] When we are convinced beyond argument that we are always right, and there is nothing more to learn, we enter a rut, and a rut is nothing but a grave with both ends kicked out.

Look into the eyes of a caged tiger at a zoo and you will see a hollow emptiness. He is a mere shadow of his former self. The big cat that once roamed freely is now staring blankly at his door, waiting for scraps of meat to be thrown into his pen. The certainty of his daily schedule has gutted him of fury and fight. A nine to five schedule may work well at the office, but it is death to the spiritual life. When we trust in the certainties that we know, we are no longer trusting the God who surprises us.

Jesus told his disciples greater works than these shall you do because I go to my Father.[35] Living in the spirit of coddiwomple is the way to achieve those greater works. Good fortune, or perhaps I should say, God fortune, favors the brave. So, let us set our sails and look to the skies to see which direction the winds will blow. A ship tied to a dock will never catch a current. Following God means that we follow the path he has placed before us no matter the outcome. As we awake each morning, we are ready to hear his directives. It is the most exciting way to live.

The first century church was a dangerous place for Christians because of a man named Saul. Having received authority from the Sanhedrin this young, aggressive rabbi set out for Damascus for the purpose of imprisoning and killing Christians. As he crested the hill, he looked down upon the city, savoring what was about to happen. Saul believed it was his mission from God to stamp out the heresy that was initiated by the Carpenter from Nazareth. God had different plans. A bright light from Heaven struck him down and blinded him. After a short conversation with Jesus, Saul wandered into the city and ended up in the home of a man named Judas. A disciple named Ananias was told to go find Saul and open his eyes to the truth. Busy packing his bags, Ananias was startled. It took a little persuasion, but the Lord finally convinced Ananias to go pray with the man he feared. Saul's eyes were opened, and the persecutor became the apostle, Paul. Ananias would have never had the joy of seeing the predator become the prey if he had tucked tail and ran for the hills. Never again did Saul walk according to his own blueprint.

Although we try to plan out our days, there is so much that we cannot control in this life. Situations at work, frustrations at home and people who come into our lives, are just a few examples of things beyond our ability to govern. There is one element, though, firmly within your grasp. It is your perspective and the attitude that follows close behind. We tend to see life from our own viewpoint or through the eyes of others. I would suggest you reject both and consider a third option. Begin to see life from God's vantage point. God is in complete control of the wind and currents. The rutter is in better hands when he guides it. Choosing to view life, with the good hand of God in control, is empowering. He sits in the heavens and never makes a mistake.

I recently spoke with a good friend whose third child has autism. He shared the family's struggles but then spoke of the goodness of God. The Lord directed them to a new community of faith where they received the support needed to raise their sweet little girl. The depth God has brought to that family, through life's surprise, was apparent. They are now walking confidently forward to a destination yet unknown, and it has reinvigorated their lives.

There is nothing certain in this life other than God. All that he wants to do in this world he does through those willing to follow his cues and obey his directives. It is not the thought of the adventurer nor the child of God to sit on the sidelines of life and watch others do battle. The victories God has rendered in our lives are but a thing of yesterday. Past triumphs are only a precursor of all he wants to do in the future. We die when we stop looking for the next open door. When we sit down and finger through the photograph albums of yesterday's blessings, we are closing the possibility of future conquests.

Coddiwomple is walking each day with a loose plan in hand and a listening ear to the Spirit. It is allowing the Lord to order our days, and thus, orchestrate our lives. There is so much unknown in the journey ahead, but he knows the path which is best. Looking back, we will see his unseen hand guiding our every step. By the way, I met my beautiful wife soon after I arrived in Mayport. Let the coddiwomple begin.

☙

Whatever your hand finds to do, do it with your might, for there is no work or thought or knowledge or wisdom in Sheol, to which you are going.

ECCLESIASTES 9:10 ESV

CHAPTER 8

Mountain Pass

P eter's life and livelihood had always been on the water. Sunrises on the Sea of Galilee, as well as the sound of its tide slapping the shoreline, were a part of his experience from a young age. Peter was more comfortable in a boat than anywhere else, and he had seen more than his share of storms. He knew that in a matter of minutes, the wind, howling down through the channels of the mountains, could whip the waves into a frenzy. However, these dangers only heightened his sense of adventure. Fishing was in his blood. The feel of the net in his hands was as natural as breathing. He understood the life of a fisherman, but things had become quite different since deciding to follow Jesus. The sea was quickly losing its charm. The excitement of the big catch had been replaced by something he was only beginning to understand. He was being called to fish in new waters and for a very different kind of catch.

Crossing over the lake with the other disciples after a day of ministry, he wished Jesus had come with them. The crowd needed to be dismissed, and so, Jesus had stayed on the shore to make sure they were all safely on their way home. The Master had also mentioned spending some time in prayer that night on the mountain which overlooked the lake. Peter looked back over his shoulder to see if he could spot Jesus against the night sky, but the sun had descended, and the moon was covered with clouds. He was becoming increasingly lonely whenever Jesus was away.

While most of the disciples were sleeping in the boat, Peter began to hear the howling of the wind. Gathering the rigging he awoke the other men. Scrambling into position, the disciples soon failed to gain control of the ship, but these were not the kind of men to give up easily. They labored on with all the strength they could muster. Soon, Peter and the other men were exhausted. Looking up they saw a man walking on the water. Thinking it was a ghost, they cried out in horror. Thomas shouted that the death angel had come to bury them in a watery grave. Judas grabbed the money bag and held it close to his chest. James hugged his younger brother, John, and assured him that they would make it to the shore somehow.

Suddenly, the ghostly figure came closer and identified himself. "It is I, be not afraid," Jesus said.[36] Fearful, the men collapsed in awe, but Peter remained standing. "If it's you," he replied. "Then let me come." Jesus, no doubt, smiled. "Come," he simply answered.[37] Stepping out onto the rolling waves, with the wind and rain beating him in the face, Peter was amazed. He was actually walking on the water until he realized he was actually walking on the water. Everything at that point went south. The record does not tell us how many steps the big fisherman took before he began to sink, but it does shed light on why he began to plummet into the deep. Peter took his eyes off the Master. He began to look at the storm instead of the Savior. Peter offered the shortest prayer in the Bible, "Lord, save me." Isn't it interesting how short and simple our prayer life becomes when our backs are pinned against the wall?

Karen and I recently returned from a vacation in the Tennessee Mountains. The colors of the trees were spectacular and the ride up, for the most part, was pleasant. My old high school buddy, Doug, had contacted me and it was good to reunite. We also shared time with our daughter's family which made it very special for both of us. But the trip was not without incident, or should I say, adventure.

Arriving in Pigeon Forge, we made a pitstop at the local grocery store. I was following my son-in-law in the hope that I would not get lost on the mountain roads. This is where good intention turned into desperate straits. Leaving the parking lot, we somehow got separated. Rather than allow the situation to overtake me, I turned to my trusty smart phone and typed in the cabin's coordinates. Up popped the GPS and off we went. After an unsuccessful ice cream diversion, we began to climb the mountain passes. Now looking back, I do not know whether the nice lady was steering me wrong, or if I wasn't following her directions. Before long, we were hopelessly lost. As most men do in these heralding situations, I did something that made no sense at all. I found the steepest driveway I could and climbed it. Sitting at the top of the driveway, I realized that the only choice I had was to back down onto the country road.

As we descended, Karen began to pray fervently. Following the script in *National Lampoon's Christmas Vacation* she cried out, "Our Father, who art in heaven, forgive my husband, for he knows not what he does." At the conclusion of her prayer, I gave a resounding *Amen,* and promptly slid off into a ditch. With my foot on the brake and my heart in my throat, I hung on for dear life. Teeter tottering off the side of the ditch I told Karen to get out of the car. If I was going to be launched into a six-foot ditch vertically, I was determined to suffer the indignity alone. I called my son-in-law in the hope that he could find me, but his GPS was working as well as mine and with my phone's battery running out, I knew I was in trouble.

In situations beyond our ability to handle, we are left with little but prayer and that is the best place to be. Sitting in the car I thought to myself, Lord I need help, and help was not far away. Several pick-up trucks stopped on the road, and men began to surround my Subaru. Realizing my front right tire was off the ground, several of them sat down on my hood while the others got behind the car. With the help of those men, my all-wheel drive, and the good Lord, I drove out of that ditch with no damage to the car. By that time, a crowd had gathered as women applauded and men cheered our victorious deliverance from the pit of disaster.

Peter gets a lot of bad press for sinking that day, but he was the only man who got out of the boat to come to Jesus. The faith it took to ignore the storm and step out of that ship was enormous, but so was the love he had for Jesus Christ. He could have waited a few moments for Jesus to get into the boat, but seconds matter when love calls. Peter was not trying to impress anyone; he just wanted to get to Jesus. The Master did not need, nor did Peter have time for, a lengthy prayer bathed in eloquent phrases and dried off with rich theological terms. "Lord, save me," was enough.[38]

The other day I asked my four-year-old granddaughter to say grace. She smiled and bowed her head and prayed, "Jesus, amen." The food on the table will never get cold when Addie prays. Although her prayer was short, the Lord looked upon it as powerful because it came from her heart. It is with the heart of a child that our Lord wants us to come to him every day. He wants us to cry out to him in our distress. Jesus delights in reassuring us of his presence. The Lord is good to all of us, and, as for me and my house, we're keeping our feet in the Florida sand for a while.

〇〰〇

Oh, taste and see that the Lord is good! Blessed is the man who takes refuge in him!

PSALM 34:8 ESV

CHAPTER 9

The Mad Hatter

The phrase, "mad as a hatter," is from the 19th century. It originated from a medical condition brought on by using mercury compound in the making of fine hats. Long exposure to this chemical often resulted in giving the hatmaker symptoms of mercury poisoning. These symptoms included tremors and mood swings. A hatter, who had worked long at his craft, would at times, appear to be a bit off his rocker. It is a bit of sad history, but true. Fortunately, today the process of making hats is much safer.

Through the centuries, people have worn hats for a variety of reasons. For ladies, it is usually fashion, but for men, they were commonly worn to cover a bald spot or shade them from the sun in the field. Hats are also used on occasion to communicate a message. Such was the case while shopping in the produce section at my grocery store. I glanced over the avocados and saw a man's cap that caught my attention. In fact, I had to look at the man's hat four times. There appeared to be a word missing, and I had to be sure it wasn't there. With a heavy heart, I concluded that the word, *not,* was indeed absent. The hat read: God is Dead.

I was saddened to see a man wearing such a statement on his hat. Furthermore, his cap sat on a head that had been given to him by God, whom he claimed was dead. After observing him pick through the oranges, I went about my business, but I'll admit that the message on the hat bothered me. I wanted to ask him what had happened that would cause him to wear such a cap. Perhaps, God did not *come through* for him in a moment of crisis or answer one of his prayers. Whatever it was, something ticked him off concerning God. I also wanted to tell him that I didn't believe him. He no more believed God was dead than he believed the orange he held in his hand was an apple. Men who really believe that God is dead don't wear hats announcing it. No one punches into the wind or throws insults into an empty cave. The man believed God was very much alive, and he was mad as tar at him.

Throughout our lives, we have all been angry at God from time to time. At times his decisions seem as cold as frozen steel, and the roadblocks he sets up smacks us in the face. We have all wrestled with being let down by the One who loves us. At other moments, it feels like he is a million miles away. Our reaction to God, though, when he exercises his divine providence in a way we do not like or understand, reveals much about us. When he clearly says no to something we desperately want, our response exposes our spiritual maturity or lack thereof. Disappointment is where the rubber meets the road on our journey to the celestial city. Moses ran into such a situation. He encountered a roadblock when it came time to enter the Promise Land.

As the children of Israel were on their way to the land of milk and honey, they were giving Moses a hard time. They were tired and thirsty, and their constant complaining wore him down. He became so angry that he struck a rock instead of speaking to it as the Lord had commanded.[39] This occurred at Meribah-Kadesh in the Desert of Zin. It seems like a small matter, but it was a big deal to the Lord for this very good reason. The rock in the wilderness was meant to be a picture of Christ. The first time the Israelites passed by the rock, Moses was told to strike it with his rod and water would flow out. The second time, he was told to speak to the rock, and then that same water would supply their need. It was a beautiful illustration of the flowing fountain of Jesus Christ.

In the first instance, the rock was struck picturing the crucifixion. In the second, all that it took to receive the water of life was to speak to the rock. Striking the rock, the first time, points to his death. There is no need for Christ to be crucified again. All that is required is faith on the part of those who kneel before the rock of Christ. We speak in faith, and the water of life flows into our souls. In essence, Moses blurred one of the pictures that God desired for us to see.

As a result, of his momentary outburst and disobedience, Moses was told he could not enter the Promise Land. He had lost his temper, and it cost him dearly. For that one moment of anger, Moses lost his dream of entering Canaan. Imagine all those years in the wilderness waiting for something that was never going to happen for him. He had given his life to lead God's people, and now he would be denied his great moment in the sun. The situation seemed terribly unfair. Bitterness was a real option for the man who had split the Red Sea and received the Ten Commandments from the hand of God himself. No one would have blamed him if he decided to throw his rod down and sputter a bit.

Instead, Moses chose higher ground. The man, who had walked with God through desert and wilderness, decided not to allow his failure at Meribah-Kadesh to define him for future generations. Moses wanted to be remembered for something grander than becoming a resentful old man. So, he decided to preach a sermon, which is recorded in the book of Deuteronomy called the *Blessing of Moses*.[40]

The location of the sermon was the wilderness beyond the river Jordan, and the moment was just before Israel entered the land under the leadership of Joshua. Even though he was being blocked from achieving his life's dream, Moses still ministered to God's people. He continued preaching. There was no hint of resentment in Moses as he focused on strengthening the Israelite nation. Moses never allowed God's *no* to cause him to become bitter and resentful. In his disappointment he discovered a precious truth. Moses preached, "To you it was shown, that you might know that the LORD is God; there is no other besides him. Out of heaven he let you hear his voice, that he might discipline you. And on earth he let you see his great fire, and you heard his words out of the midst of the fire. And because he loved your fathers and chose their offspring after them and brought you out of Egypt with his own presence, by his great power."[41] Canaan was not the ultimate treasure to be gained; it was God himself who was his prized possession. God took away the lesser to give Moses the greatest gift.

When the things we desire become more important than God himself, he is ruthless at taking them away. When our dreams become bigger than our relationships, the Lord has a habit of pulling the rug out from underneath us. He does not do this with the cold calculation of a distant deity. God desires our greatest good, and many times we are just too blind to see it. The man in the hat had something taken away from him, and he was angry. He wanted others to think God was dead when he himself knew it was a lie. Again, you don't take a swing at a corpse. God was trying to get his attention, and it would not be a surprise to someday learn that he has surrendered his life to Jesus Christ. C.S. Lewis, by his own admission, came like, "a prodigal who is brought in kicking, struggling, resentful, and darting his eyes in every direction for a chance of escape."[42] The man whose hat read, *God is Dead*, was being pursued by the Hound of Heaven. God, who spared not his own Son, will stop at nothing to bring us to himself. He will strip away anything that keeps us away from him because of the intensity of his love. The sooner you put up the white flag of surrender, the quicker you will be surprised by joy.

⟨ↂ⟩

And to the angel of the church in Pergamum write: 'The words of him who has the sharp two-edged sword.

REVELATION 2:12 ESV

CHAPTER 10

The Grove

Solomon was a hopeless romantic. In his memoirs, *Song of Solomon*, he reveals his passionate love for a woman named Abishag. It is believed she was the young woman who laid by King David in his old age, when he needed warmth. Solomon fell in love watching this young woman take such good care of his dying father. Her deep respect for the King touched Solomon's heart. According to the Bible, Solomon had 700 wives and 300 concubines, but he had only one true love.[43] He told his beloved, "Set me as a seal upon your heart, as a seal upon your arm, for love is strong as death, jealousy is fierce as the grave. Its flashes are flashes of fire, the very flame of the LORD."[44] Solomon was asking her to pledge her loyalty and devotion to him because to do any less would wreak havoc on his love-sick heart. As the old saying goes, *Ain't love grand*.

The film, *Love Is a Many-Splendored Thing*, first debuted in 1955. It involved an American reporter, played by William Holden, who fell in love with a Eurasian doctor, played by Jennifer Jones. I must confess I have never actually watched the movie, but the title has always intrigued me. *Love is a Many-**Splintered** Thing* seems like a more fitting title. True, love provides moments of glorious splendor, when the moon shines bright and cuts a glowing cast across our loved one's delicate face. There are times when all is well in our feathered love nest. Likewise, all of us have experienced friendships that we counted closer than a brother. However, there are moments when loving someone is a raw and ready choice. The grit involved to keep relationships growing requires more than just the emotion of love.

In every loving relationship there are times of deep distress that test our resolve to just stay in the game. In these periods, when love drives us insane and relationships are strained, something deeper must prevail to keep love and friendships alive. There is a common thread that binds us together and keeps us from destroying the relationships we so greatly value. Mutual respect for our differences is the secret to weathering the storms; it is the foundational block of a growing relationship. When we forget to respect others, we violate boundaries by saying or doing things that offend. Maintaining that kind of respect is the underpinning that must support the structure of our friendships, or those relationships will collapse like a bamboo hut in a hurricane. Love grows in the soil of respecting the rights of others to feel and think differently. With that thought in mind, I offer the following parable…,

Once upon a time, in a land far away, there was a beautiful valley. Lush vegetation covered its gentle slopes, and the stream that ran through it sang a happy song. But alas, all was not well in the valley, for it had no trees. As a result, a general air of sadness rested in the sweet flag blossoms, and an unspoken gloom caused butterfly wings to droop. Birds came to feast on the seeds of the sunflowers, but none stayed to build nests and raise their young. Travelers stopped to drink from the brook, but none built homes for lack of shade. And then, one day, the Tree Planter arrived. As he sat on a rock overlooking the green valley he began to weep. *I shall fill this valley with trees*, he thought. Picking up his satchel of seeds, he carefully planted trees of many different varieties throughout the valley. Having completed his task, the Tree Planter smiled and continued on his journey.

Weeks turned into months, as the tiny seedlings began to sprout and grow. Within a few short years, all the trees of the valley were strong with limbs and leaves that reached toward heaven. In these early days, each tree embraced the beauty of their fellow sapling, reveling in the diversity they shared. The apple tree considered the pear tree a thing of wonder, fascinated by the shape of its light green fruit. The young oak thought that the bark of the birch was exquisite, often commenting on its color and texture. The maple loved the massive green leaves of the sycamore. The sycamore, in turn, enjoyed the sweet fragrance of the sap that ran down the trunk of the maple. They all celebrated each other's uniqueness.

Then, one day, a swarm of locusts flew into the valley. Boring into the bark of the trees, they laid their eggs and then flew off to infect other groves. Unnoticed, the eggs hatched and began to poison each tree with a disease call Pride. The sickness caused them to forget their own value, and so, they devalued one another. Before long the trees of the valley began to change. No longer did they esteem their fellow trees with high dignity and grace. Where once they rejoiced in their diversity, now those same differences irritated them. In fact, they began to envy and despise one another. The apple tree gossiped about the pear tree, commenting on the ridiculous shape of its fruit. The towering oak looked down on the smaller elm, pointing out, for all who would listen, how much taller it was then that *insignificant* little elm tree. She even threatened to fall on the elm if it said a cross word. The maple became annoyed at the sycamore's huge crusty leaves, which gathered at her base. *Messy tree*, she thought. Animosity spread like a canker throughout the grove, and as a result, the trees began to turn away from one another.

One day, the Tree-Planter returned to see how his grove of trees fared. Cresting the hill, he could not believe his eyes. All the trees he had planted were dying. He instantly knew what had had happened and began to weep. *Do they not understand that their beauty is in their diversity*, cried out the Tree-Planter? *If I had planted the grove with all the same trees, how boring and ugly the valley would have been. And yet, look at it now. It is dying before my eyes. My trees have forgotten they were all planted by the same hand and that their beauty was in the unique design I had given them.*

To see the value and beauty in another person, one must embrace and celebrate how God has made them. We must never attempt to remake them in our own image. By attempting to mold another person to our liking, we forget that they were created in the image of God. The Lord has created us all with unique personalities, different interests, and diverse temperaments. Every person deserves to be loved for who they are, not how we believe they should think and behave. When we view those closest to us as projects instead of people, we devalue them. We communicate, in subtle ways, that they are not enough and that there is something inherently wrong with them.

Paul wrote concerning love, "Love is patient and kind; love does not envy or boast; it is not arrogant or rude. It does not insist on its own way; it is not irritable or resentful. Love bears all things, believes all things, hopes all things, endures all things."[45] Love is a lot of hard work but let me assure you after forty years of loving the same woman, it is well worth it. The relationship we share grows deeper every day because we have fought for the love we treasure. We have accepted the fact that we are different, and we are stronger for it.

ᏣᎳᎦ

Love is patient and kind; ...

1 CORINTHIAN 13:4 ESV

CHAPTER 11

Right Thinking

I n 1903, James Allen published a book titled, *As a Man Thinketh*. Lifting a phrase from Proverbs twenty-three, Allen twisted its meaning to propagate his false teaching on the power of the mind. He described his writing as, "A book that will help you to help yourself," and, "a book on the power and right application of thought."[46] James Allen was the father of self-help gurus and the inspiration for later writers such as Norman Vincent Peale, Joseph Murphy, and Stephan Richards. Sold world-wide, this book has led millions down a path of darkness and deception. The author deifies the mind, misleading his readers by suggesting they have the power to create whatever reality they desire with their minds. He opens his book with this statement, *"Mind is the Master power that molds and makes, And Man is Mind, and evermore he takes The tool of Thought, and, shaping what he wills, Brings forth a thousand joys, a thousand ills: - He thinks in secret, and it comes to pass: Environment is but his looking-glass."*[47]

Although this quote might sound powerful and appealing to some, Allen's work crumbles on two distinct fault lines. Firstly, God created the heavens and the earth; therefore, he is the starting place if a man is to discover the meaning and purpose of life. Creation is making something out of nothing, and this is clearly the prerogative of God. In the purest sense of the word, man creates nothing, much less his own world. Mankind, for all his efforts, is powerless to change reality. If you stand out in the rain, you will get wet, and no amount of mind-control will keep you dry. Man is more than *mind*; he is made in the image of God and can no more change that reality than a leopard can change his spots, or an elephant grow an extra trunk.

Secondly, the mind of man has been crippled by sin. As a result of sin, man has become hopelessly introspective, and therefore, any conclusion he comes to is a cat chasing its own tail. Man is attempting to knock down bowling pins with a cracked and warped bowling ball, and as a result, all his thoughts inevitably end up in the gutter. A toaster plugged into itself cannot burn a piece of bread, and a man disconnected from his Creator cannot think clearly. He views reality through a broken window, seeing shadows rather than clear images. Even the attempt to change his reality through his mind reveals a deep ignorance toward his own being and abilities.

The fact that James Allen uses the Bible as the basis of his deception reveals an old strategy of Satan when he approached Eve in the garden, "Hath God said, Ye shall not eat of every tree of the garden?"[48] When Solomon wrote, "As a man thinks in his heart, so is he,"[49], he did not mean what Allen proposes. The verse is speaking of an evil man who invites someone to his table to share a delicious meal for the purpose of entrapping him. "Eat and drink," he says. "But his heart is not with you."[50] It is a warning not to eat with an evil man lest you vomit the food you have eaten. The host smiles and offers more peas all the while plotting the downfall of his unsuspecting guest. Now it is true that our mind is powerful, so, let's consider why God gave us an intellect in the first place.

Among all our faculties the mind is one of our most useful tools. How we think affects our choices and behavior. Our view of life is largely seen through the lens of our minds, and so, right thinking is vital to right living. Also, God would not have given us such a marvelous instrument if he did not intend for us to use it. The Bible is not silent concerning the importance of correct thought patterns. Paul gave the Philippians a laundry list of the finer things of life and then told them to think on these things.[51] Paul tells the Romans not to be conformed to this world but transformed by the renewing in your mind.[52] Paul goes so far as to say that we have the mind of Christ. What we fill our minds with has a tremendous affect, but there is something deeper to be considered. The mind is powerful, but not in the way Allen teaches.

In the natural realm, we gain knowledge through curiosity. We examine evidence in the natural world and come to certain conclusions. This is healthy and good, but it does nothing to lift us out of our corporate misery. Within any of these avenues, man's attempt to advance his intellect is weighted down by a heavy anchor. He is trying to think his way to a better life apart from the source of all wisdom and knowledge. The necessary requirement is a full reversal in the way we think and occurs when a man is born again.

Once a person receives the foundation of a spiritual life, being Christ, that individual can begin to receive facts that are beyond their ability to understand, and yet, are true. "We have to let our brains be guided by the Holy Spirit into thinking a great many things we have not experienced. That is, we are committed to Jesus Christ's view of everything and if we only allow our brains to dwell on what we have experienced, we shut ourselves off from a great deal we ought to be exercised in."[53] Once the Spirit of God enters the equation, a new way of thinking can be established. A new foundation has been poured in our soul for the purpose of building a new way of thinking about ourselves and life. The broken window has been replaced, and we now look through a new piece of glass. There is, though, a process to be considered.

No one is born with great character, high integrity, or a thriving mind. These things must be developed over time through discipline and choice. The young schoolgirl who studies diligently and refuses to entertain gossip is on her way to a good life. In the same way, the spiritual life must be developed over time by discipline and choice on a new set of facts. The life of Jesus enters us in its fullness with the need to be developed. Just as a seed holds the entire life of a plant in its small shell, the spiritual life has been given to us in seed form. The essential thing is to reject the old patterns of thinking and embrace a new reality based on *revelation* facts. These facts are found in Scripture, and they run contrary to the natural realm. Common sense facts are replaced by a higher set of truths. Consider the following example.

In the book of 1 John, this truth is stated, "God is love," and yet, everything in our world points in the opposite direction. If God is love, the skeptic will claim, then why is there suffering, tragedy, and heartache. If God is love, then why did he put Adam and Eve in a garden and offer them forbidden fruit? Empirical evidence runs counter to John's theological position, and yet, in the face of all these apparent contradictions, the Scripture boldly proclaims that God *is* love. It is easy to draw this conclusion from our limited perspective. However, right thinking begins when we reject our rational mind in the light of biblical truth. If what we understand as being true is contradicted by the Scripture, then we must make a choice. We must reject our skewed understanding based on our rational mind before we can embrace biblical truth. The truth of God's love for the world is an example of a revelation fact, which must be received by faith.

The choice to believe always precedes our understanding. We believe; therefore, we think.

Freedom and victory enter when we trust God's declarations of truth over our own conclusions in life. This is what the Scripture means when it declares, "So faith comes from hearing, and hearing through the word of Christ."[54] We only begin to think clearly when we are seeing things from God's perspective. James Allen was wrong concerning the proper use of the mind. In fact, he had it all backwards. Environment is not man's looking glass that he can adjust through the power of the mind. Environment is the domain of God, and all the changes are made in our lives by his sovereign hand. Simply put, he is God, and we are not. The whole foundation of our thinking is not based on how we think, but our faith in who we believe. "We have the mind of Christ."[55]

ᏊᎢᏊᏡᎧ

Finally, brethren, whatsoever things are true..., think on these things.

PHILIPPIANS 4:8 ESV

CHAPTER 12

Barefoot in the Desert

In my carefree days of adolescence, I lived for three things: summer break, the county fair, and going barefoot when the weather warmed. I remember throwing my sneakers in the corner, pulling off my socks, and heading out in search of adventure. In those days parents rarely knew where their kids were, and I loved the freedom autonomy gave me. My friends and I would head for the hills and streams to fight dragons and seek our fortunes. At first, my tender feet screamed at every pebble, but within a few days, my dogs would be as tough as rawhide. I often wish we could go back to those fun days of *summers without shoes*. Comfortable socks and arch supports are for old men and old women.

Going barefoot has become a lost art. In the present age of germ phobia, the thought of bare skin on the rugged ground sends chills up the spine of most parents. Children today are missing one of the pure pleasures of life by not going barefoot. Today's young people will never know the sensation of stepping into a cow patty and feeling that warm bovine excrement ooze between their toes. They will never feel the adrenaline rush brought on by stepping on a bed of thorns. Regardless of the danger of invisible, bloodsucking parasites burying themselves under our toenails, I would like to suggest we all unlace our shoes, throw them in the corner, and go outside for a stroll in the meadow. You might find it to be a spiritual moment, just as Moses experienced.

While tending sheep in the desert, Moses came across a burning bush.[56] A plant on fire in a hot desert was not an unusual sight. The blazing desert sun, along with the dryness of the vegetation, caused such things to occur on a regular basis. This, though, was no ordinary bush. As hot as the fire burned, the bush was not consumed. As Moses came closer, a voice commanded him to remove his shoes because the ground he was standing on was holy ground. In deep reverence, he exposed his feet to the rugged terrain of the desert.

An ordinary day watching his father-in-law's sheep suddenly became a sacred moment. In the most unexpected place Moses discovered the joy of God's unfiltered presence. Why would the Lord choose such an unusual way to reveal himself? A common plant in which to place his fiery presence seems like such an unworthy vessel. A rock or large tree would make more sense. A mountain would be more majestic. Instead, he chose a dry bush and for a very specific reason.

The future deliverer of Israel had been out in the wilderness tending sheep for forty years. His own personal exodus out of Egypt was a surprising plot twist for a man who was destined for greatness in the most powerful nation on earth. Moses had been brought up in the house of Pharoah with the intent of becoming a prince of Egypt. He was on the fast track to the throne. His trajectory to the top of the social and political structure of the land of the Pharaohs was cut short when he murdered an Egyptian. Escaping with his life, Moses ended up on the backside of a desert, married to the daughter of a sheepherder named Jethro. Following sheep around in the desert for that many years doesn't exactly stimulate the intellect and boost personal confidence. Being a sheepherder had become his identity. God needed to redefine Moses' life with new parameters and a new direction. He needed a new identity.

The source of the fire Moses was witnessing was not the bush, it was God *in* the bush. Man was created to be filled with the fiery presence of his Maker. Apart from God we are a dry twig in a desert of loneliness. We appear to be strong when we are quite weak. Moses needed to recognize that the fire of God burns brightest through human frailty. God did not need an up-and-coming star to lead his people out of Egypt, he chose to use a lonely sheepherder.

Before leaving Egypt, Moses had great confidence in his own ability to lead the children of Israel out of bondage. The killing of the Egyptian was Moses' attempt to defend God's people. A man's personal strengths, though, are never used in the kingdom of God. Moses needed to see how weak he was so that he would not trust in himself. "But we have this treasure in jars of clay, to show that the surpassing power belongs to God and not to us."[57] When the burning presence of God fills our *barefoot* vulnerability, our frailty becomes God's opportunity. He consumes us with his presence. This was the reason God revealed himself in the burning bush.

To be used by God requires humility, but there comes a point when humility can turn against us. We can begin to define ourselves by our greatest failure rather than by God's presence. Strange as it might sound, humility turns into a subtle source of pride. God, though, was persistent. "For the gifts and the calling of God are irrevocable."[58]

When God revealed his plan for Moses to return and deliver his people, the once strong and confident young man of Egypt stuttered and stammered. He complained that he couldn't put a decent sentence together. Apparently, talking to sheep for forty years had affected his ability to communicate on a human level. The years in the desert humbled Moses, maybe a little too much. He needed to take his eyes off himself and place them on an all-powerful God.

During my years of ministry, I have seen God use the most unusual people to do his work. I recall a man who was deaf in one ear working in our sound booth for years. A young woman who was terrified to speak in public has become one of our best conference speakers. A painter, injured in his trade, has become our best cook in the church kitchen, and the list goes on.

When the Lord calls us to follow him, he accepts no excuses. He is not counting on our abilities; he is waiting for our willingness to trust him. The fire he places in us burns brightest when we see our own frailty. When his holiness and fire invade us, we brilliantly burn with his glory. It is the fire of the Holy Spirit that others need to see, not the bush. When that happens, God receives all the glory.

⚭

Then he said, "Do not come near; take your sandals off your feet, for the place on which you are standing is holy ground."

EXODUS 3:5 ESV

CHAPTER 13

A Watery Gospel

Ray Kinsella was a farmer from Iowa who heard voices in his cornfield. He was told, "If you build it, they will come." So, Ray built a ballfield, and they came. Ball players from long ago led by none other than Shoeless Joe Jackson walked out of the cornfields and onto the diamond. As the ball players emerged from the cornfield each evening, Ray watched his hard work and dreams pay off. *Shoeless Joe* was written in 1982, by W.P. Kinsella, and soon after became a major motion picture, *Field of Dreams.* Hearing voices in a cornfield usually gets a man a visit from the local shrink, but in Ray's case it ended up fulfilling his dreams. You might be interested to know that listening to voices that lead men down strange paths is not exclusive to Kinsella's novel. It has been happening in the church for thousands of years.

The Devil has been whispering in the ears of false preachers for centuries to preach half-truths and feel-good messages to build their congregations. He's been telling them to proclaim a message of selfish indulgence to have sinners flock to their door. The Devil tells them they can prophesy their destiny with their own words, and people will come. He tells them to turn a blind eye to sin and people will applaud them, their building will be packed, and their offerings will burst all expectations. However, success in the eyes of men is almost always failure in the courts of Heaven. If packed out buildings and overflowing offering plates is a barometer of success, then these men are certainly on the right path. The question is, where does that path lead? What men call gold, silver, and precious metal, is nothing more than wood, hay, and stubble. J. Vernon McGee said it well, "there's an awful lot of fellows out there building big haystacks."

Considering this dilemma of spiritual dystopia, the question before the church today remains the same as it was in the first century. Will she sacrifice the true gospel for a more comfortable and pleasing message? The church is always in danger of compromising its message for worldly gain. For the sake of a bigger crowd the church has always been tempted to adopt a watered-down gospel. A generation of itching ears demands a more palatable message. The Greeks of the first and second century infiltrated the church with a heresy called Gnosticism. They attempted to mix the mysticism of special knowledge with the truth of the gospel. Like a cockroach in a glass of sweet tea, they contaminated the message. Thankfully, in the first century, the warnings of the apostle John steered the church into safer waters. What was dangerous in the first century has become deadly in these last days.

In the book of Revelation, Jesus confronted the church of Laodicea with this stinging rebuke, "For you say, I am rich, I have prospered, and I need nothing, not realizing that you are wretched, pitiable, poor, blind, and naked."[59] They were neither hot nor cold. They were doing ministry in that mushy middle of lukewarmness which made him sick to his stomach. Their preaching sounded no different than the world's call to self-centered narcissism.

Packaged in spiritual wrapping and tied with the bow of biblical sounding phrases, the church today offers a poisonous mix of delusion and lies. Many preach that the gospel is all about their prosperity and happiness. You can finally fulfill your *field of dreams* with the help of a benevolent god. The Lord spoke through the prophet Ezekiel, rebuking preachers who preached and lived for their own indulgences, "Son of man, prophesy against the shepherds of Israel; prophesy, and say to them, even to the shepherds, Thus says the Lord GOD: Ah, shepherds of Israel who have been feeding yourselves! Should not shepherds feed the sheep?"[60]

The true gospel wounds the sinner to cure them with the healing message of forgiveness and redemption. The church of Laodicea had no interest in preaching a message that offended its congregants. We have lived into such a day. The modern pulpit has become a place of pep talks and weak, sterile theology. The thundering, *Thus saith the Lord*, is strange to the ears of most church goers in these last days. Pulpits across the land offer a warm breeze rather than a mighty wind, a flickering flame rather than the roaring inferno of truth. Of the seven churches that Jesus addressed in Revelation, he held out the least hope for Laodicea. He confirmed his love for this church and as a result promised a rebuke. Jesus counseled them to buy gold, tried in the fire. He desired them to dress in the white robe of righteousness. He told them to reject the wood, hay, and stubble and embrace the precious gold of eternal truth. He offered an open door to any individual that would hear his voice and promised intimacy and a seat near the throne of God. John wrote this concerning the church of Laodicea, "The one who conquers, I will grant him to sit with me on my throne, as I also conquered and sat down with my Father on his throne."[61]

John refused to be silent concerning the gospel; therefore, he was exiled to the island of Patmos. The Romans had had enough of the old man and were attempting to silence him. The gospel he preached offended them, and he suffered as a result. The true message from Heaven will always be offensive to this world, but it is its only hope. As Oswald Chambers once said, "The church confronts the world with a message the world craves for but resents because it comes through the cross of Christ."[62] To compromise the ideals of the gospel and adopt a worldly mentality is Satanic at its core. Pandering to the culture to reach the culture is an old ploy. These preachers insist, "Sin is not anarchy, it is a disease. Men are not in rebellion against God, they just need to know how much you love them. Win them with love, not a cross. Don't insist that men must be born again, they just need you to help them a bit. Abandon the cross and all this talk of redemption, and the kingdoms of the world will be ours for the taking. Offer them a watered-down gospel where social justice is the theme with little mention of men needing to be saved from sin."

The church of the Laodicean age that we are presently witnessing, has embraced those lies and sold her soul to the enemy. She is making empty promises to her children that lead to nothing more than disillusionment and despondency. "I counsel you to buy from me gold refined by fire, so that you may be rich, and white garments so that you may clothe yourself and the shame of your nakedness may not be seen, and salve to anoint your eyes, so that you may see."[63] The gospel of the Lord Jesus Christ is the only one that can truly satisfy our souls, and it is our only true *field of dreams.*

GMMO

And he said to him, "All these will I give you,
if you will fall down and worship me."

MATTHEW 4:9 ESV

CHAPTER 14

The Debate

I t is a debate that has raged for centuries. Each generation picks up where the last left off with little to show for their efforts. With heels dug in, neither concede any ground as they lob Molotov cocktails from their perspective foxholes. I am speaking about the endless discussion concerning the sovereignty of God versus the free will of man regarding salvation. To put it simply, did he choose us, or do we choose him? To those who have marched down this slippery slope, the names of John Calvin and Jacob Arminian are familiar. Relationships between brothers dissolve into dust when the battle reaches a fevered pitch, and the church again is divided needlessly. As one woman said, as she stood up in a meeting where the debate was raging, "Why can't we all just talk about Jesus?" I also wonder the same question. I want to know what all the fuss is about.

The following helps describe the battle. Arminianism argues that man freely choses Christ apart from God's choosing him. They claim that if God sovereignly choses men to be saved, then he has stripped them of their free will and created a robotic bride. Calvinism counters that God choses specific men to be saved apart from any foreknowledge of that man choosing him. This second camp argues that if men can exercise their free will to be saved, then the sovereignty of God has been violated, and now, the origin of salvation is man, not God. Both sides pound their Bibles incessantly and point to proof texts. The latter point out that we are called the elect of God, but the Bible also says, "For God so loved the world,"[64] not just the elect. The former sites one of the last verses in the Bible, "The Spirit and the Bride say, 'Come.' And let the one who hears say, 'Come.' And let the one who is thirsty come; let the one who desires take the water of life without price."[65] The Calvinist returns the volley by stating, "Salvation is of the Lord."[66] Round and round they go.., It gets thicker, but I would spare you this head-throbbing exercise.

Although I understand the tension inherent in the debate, the mindless query between these two camps gives me a headache. The language both groups use in explaining their positions requires a stack of thick, dusty theological books. They both weave together Bible verses creating a collage of opinions leading to a mosaic of monotony. Reconciling the two camps is impossible since both sides present their argument with an either-or proposition. To both, the middle ground is a mushy mess they refuse to enter. They each find it impossible to reconcile God's sovereignty and man's free will because it violates their human reasoning. Both positions cannot be equally true, they conclude. The result is that the two opposing armies reload their cannons and fire away with more Bible verses. To repeat, all this endless wrangling gives me a headache.

At this point, I do not intend to enter the debate and never will. The argument between both camps is a distraction away from the ultimate purpose of the church, which is to simply preach Christ. Both have left their first love to chase after lesser gods of their own pride and making. Rather, I would ask both sides to pause long enough to let the dust settle and consider this question. What is being accomplished for the cause of the gospel with all this strife? Sinners need a clear gospel presentation, not a treatise on the determinate will of God. Christians need to be fed first the milk and then the meat of the Word, not led down a path of division. Jesus never spent time teaching either of these opposing views. He ministered the love and truth of God to hurting and hungry people. Believers don't need the empty fortresses of theological camps, filled with gunpowder and ammo for the purpose of shooting at their brothers in Christ. What we all need is to lay down our arms and seek the riches found in Jesus Christ.

God's sovereignty does not violate our free will, and our free will does not circumvent God's choosing us. Both positions are equally taught in Scripture. They co-exist, side by side, in perfect harmony. Both groups have made rational thinking a little god. Both camps dictate, and thus limit, God's greatness, and ability. God's ways are so far above man's reasoning powers as to create a mystery so beautiful that our rational mind cannot wrap itself around it. If a man tried to stuff Heaven into his head, it would explode. I am suggesting that we embrace both positions as equally true and allow our heads to wander into the mystery of God's eternal edicts. Mystery does not violate human reasoning; it expands our limited intellects to discover knowledge outside its purview. We do not understand to believe, we believe to understand. *Whosoever*, means anyone can come to Christ and *elect*, means he has chosen those who will be saved.

In Isaiah's day, God's people had turned to idolatry. With the same block of wood, God declared, they cooked their meal and built their idol.[67] They had created a god out of their reasoning minds which satisfied their intellect. No mystery was needed as they bowed down to the idol of their hands. They could understand and control a piece of wood. The attempt of these two opposing sides to reconcile sovereignty and free will is a prideful attempt to understand God with their rational mind. It is blockhead thinking. Both camps are entertaining the false god of pride and arrogance. I am not interested in a God that I can figure out. I worship a God who both sovereignly choses; and yet, in his choosing he never violates our free will to choose him. A wooden head of rational thinking will never worship God. The debate between these two groups has destroyed their ability to worship the splendor of God.

A few months ago, I gave up eating chicken and scrambled eggs. I had become frustrated with trying to discover which came first, the chicken or the egg. I miss both, but my reasoning mind must be satisfied, and until it is, a piece of fried chicken or two-over-easy will not pass my lips. I've got my heels dug in and I refuse to budge. Although this is a simple illustration, the point is clear. We miss out on the beauty of both chicken and egg by our stubborn pride.

This debate over sovereignty and free will is a dangerous distraction. By trying to "figure out" sovereignty and free will, we fail to walk in the simplicity of Christ. Lay the debate down. In the heated exchange you are missing the wonder of Christ. You have become prideful and brainy about the whole thing. He chose you and you chose him, now rejoice over that wonderful truth. Salvation is not of man; it is of the Lord and that blessed word *whosoever* sets the parameters of who can be born again. I really don't see what all the fuss is about. Of course, I believe in free will, what choice do I have? I stand in solidarity with the woman who asked in a church meeting, "Why can't we all just talk about Jesus?"

～∞～

> He burns part of the tree to roast his meat
> and keep himself warm…Then he takes
> what's left and makes his god.

ISAIAH 44:16,17 NLT

CHAPTER 15

A Kangaroo Court

I love etymology. The study of the origin of words and phrases and how their meanings have changed over time has always fascinated me. For instance, the word *quarantine* is a French word meaning forty for the following reason. When a ship arrived at port carrying sick passengers, it was required to stay out in the harbor forty days before docking. *Bumfodder*, was the 17th century English word for toilet paper. A secondary meaning for the word, *bumfodder*, is useless writing. Ouch. The term, *kangaroo court*, came from the 1850s during the California gold rush. Mines that looked promising were quickly grabbed by speculators in the following manner. After hastily forming a court in town, the man who wanted the land in question would present false paperwork and then stake his claim. The whole exercise was for the appearance of being a legal proceeding, but it was not. Laws were broken by judges who had sworn to uphold them, and juries were quickly assembled by clearing out the saloons. These speculators jumped like kangaroos on promising mines. Smoky courtrooms were filled with those who jumped like kangaroos to make a dollar. Webster defined the phrase *kangaroo court* like this, "A mock court in which the principles of law and justice are disregarded or perverted. A court characterized by irresponsible, unauthorized, or irregular status or procedures."[68] Not surprisingly, this travesty of justice is older than the 1850s and not restricted to the region of the Old West.

The classic *kangaroo court* of the ages was held 2000 years ago in the home of Caiaphas the high priest and executed by a Jewish court called the Sanhedrin. Jesus was arrested and then transported in the middle of the night from the Garden of Gethsemane. The list of irregularities concerning his trial are too numerous to mention, but I will reference a few. The fact that the trial was held at night made it illegal. Any court proceedings in the home of Caiaphas were forbidden by Jewish law. If a man was found guilty in a Jewish court, three days had to elapse before judgment was rendered. A series of false witnesses were brought in longer than a Texas mile, and each lie they told was shot down quicker than a New York minute. The only charge that seemed to hold any water was his statement regarding destroying the temple, but even that accusation was a lie. Undoubtedly, Caiaphas's *kangaroo court* didn't care. He was so bent on a guilty verdict that he required no true evidence to convict the Son of God.

Through the ages, these types of trials have occurred, resulting in injustices. Men have had the cards stacked against them. We have all stood before men and institutions that we respected, and then for some unknown reason, they turned on us like bloodthirsty animals. Life is not fair. A careful reading of *Foxes Book of Martyrs* will open one's eyes to what believers in Jesus have endured through the centuries. Burned at the stake, tortured with hot pinchers, sewn in animal skins, and then released to wild beasts, to be torn to shreds, only begins to tell the tale of God's faithful martyrs. In all these afflictions, the true court of Heaven awaits the final judgement of the wicked officials of these *kangaroo courts*. As Francis Schaeffer titled his book, *He is there, and He is not silent.* Friedrich Von Logau said it well in his 17th century poem titled, *Retribution.* "Though the mills of God grind slowly, yet they grind exceedingly small; Though with patience he stands waiting, with exactness grind he all."[69] Examples of *kangaroo courts* abound in the Scriptures.

Eli was a priest in Israel who had two worthless sons. Regrettably, he refused to rebuke them because he was secretly enjoying the benefits of their wickedness. His sons, Hophni and Phinehas, were receiving offerings from the Lord by the hand of the Israelites. The practice went like this, the priests would stick a three-prong fork into a pot of boiling water to retrieve whatever parts of the meat therein as their portion. Whatever the prongs impaled they could keep. However, these two wicked men were demanding that the meat simply be handed over to them so that they would get a greater portion. Eli was growing fat as a result. Furthermore, there were reports throughout the land that these two men were lying with women who were serving at the tent of the meeting. These men should have been removed from the temple, but instead, Eli did nothing. Sin that is not dealt with does not dissipate; it grows.

Rather than remove his sons from the priesthood, Eli simply asked them, "Why are you doing this?"[70] A mild rebuke considering the wickedness of the situation. Eli's lackadaisical approach was a sad commentary on his duty as a father and his responsibility as the High Priest. Rather than repent, Hophni and Phineas refused to listen to the voice of their father. I can see them walking away from the meeting chuckling between themselves and thinking what a foolish old man their father had become. The old priest refused to fulfill his responsibilities to the Lord, and as a result, both of his sons were killed on the same day in battle. Eli made a mockery of his position as High Priest, dishonoring the Lord. He chose his sons over obedience to God.

When Eli was ninety-eight years old, the Ark of the Lord was stolen by the Philistines on the same day that his sons died in battle. Upon hearing the news, the old priest, now a very heavy man, fell backwards and broke his neck. His last statement: his last concern, was not for his sons who had died that day in battle, but for the Ark of the Covenant. Eli's abuse of the office of the priesthood, caused him to become numb to his own family.

When a judge chooses willfully to disobey the very laws he was sworn to uphold, then that court is no longer legitimate. The same is true of any government that refuses to defend the very laws it has established. In that moment, the whole establishment of authority breaks down into a thin façade and society spirals out of control. What would cause those in authority to stoop to such depravity? In the case of Caiaphas, and those who sat with him that night, their lust for power caused them to condemn the Son of God to death. In Eli's case, it was his abuse of his spiritual position for his own pleasure. It is no different today. How should we conduct ourselves when confronted with *kangaroo courts* in our day, whether in churches or governmental seats?

In his response to the *kangaroo court* of his day Jesus gave us direction. He was silent up to the point when they asked him who he was. He then, in unmistakable terms, declared himself to be the Son of God and the Son of Man who would return in the clouds with power and glory. The Sanhedrin, in that moment, committed the most heinous crime in history. But their evil deeds would not go unpunished, and neither will any *kangaroo court* today that continues to disobey the rule of law. The Son of Man is coming in the clouds to execute judgment. When the unrighteousness of men seems to rule the day be reassured. There is not a *kangaroo court* in this world that he is not watching, no matter where it exists. Our responsibility is to continue to proclaim Christ regardless of injustices. We will stand before the judgement seat of Christ.

⚬↬↬⚬

And they that laid hold on Jesus lead him away to Caiaphas the high priest, where the scribes and elders were assembled.

MATTHEW 26:57 KJV

CHAPTER 16

Hated for His Name's Sake

In 1970, Lynn Anderson recorded, *Rose Garden*, which included the line, *I beg your pardon, (I never promised you a rose garden)*. It soon after became one of the most popular country songs in history. In explaining its success Anderson offered this, "It was popular because it touched on emotions. It was perfectly timed. It was out just as we came out of the Vietnam years and a lot of people were trying to recover."[71] The realization that life is not always the rose garden we desire, is made clear through difficult times, through times of disappointment. Life sometimes serves up lemons.

Disappointment is unfulfilled expectations. We expected something that was not delivered. Since this is true, the only way to free ourselves from being *let down* is to embrace reality, not the façade of fluff placed before us by this world. We must return to the original contract we have with life and read it again. Life is not fair nor equitable. Or, said in a simpler way, "I never promised you a rose garden." Certainly, Jesus never did.

To further emphasize this point, there is an old saying that forewarned is forearmed. The Lord most assuredly warned his disciples of the dangers ahead if they chose to follow him. He had no desire to have them sign on the dotted line before they knew all that would be involved. Jesus said this, "If the world hates you, know that it has hated me before it hated you. If you were of the world, the world would love you as its own; but because you are not of the world, but I chose you out of the world, therefore the world hates you."[72] The Greek word *hate*, means to "despise; to actively pursue for the purpose of harming." The hatred the world has for Christians is because of their association with Jesus Christ. The core of their hateful energy is directed primarily toward our Lord for a very specific reason. When he came, he upset the apple cart, and certainly did not offer us a rose garden.

It is a reality few of us experience, and yet, it is nevertheless true. The world hates those who follow Christ. That fact may be set aside as nonexistence, but there are unseen forces flowing against us. Those forces may seem inconsequential one moment and blazingly apparent the next. Stepping into a fast-moving stream is one thing; we feel its current and know we are walking against its flow. At the same time, to be hit with a large, floating log in the chest is another matter. The former is a constant pressure to conform to this world, while the latter is a full-frontal assault from our enemy.

Now before we pull out our martyrs' cap and cry foul, let's carefully examine that supposition. Who is it who hates us and what is the source of their animosity? Understanding those two things will better position us to endure the flame of persecution when it arrives, and it will come. Paul reminded Timothy that all who lived Godly would suffer attacks from the enemy.[73]

To understand this warning let's first consider the word, *world*. In the Greek language *world* is rendered cosmos, and it can be understood in one of three ways. First, it can refer to the planet, but I've never been attacked by an apple tree, so let's mark that off our list. Secondly, the *world* can refer to people, as seen in John 3:16, "For God so loved the world." Our fellow man is the reason Jesus died, and so, humanity left to themselves must be eliminated from our options. I have had non-Christians who loved me, and Christians who moved to the other side of the street when I walked toward them.

Lastly, the word points to the world system established by our enemy, Satan. The purpose of this system is to keep men away from Christ and in bondage to sin. "In their case the god of this world has blinded the minds of the unbelievers, to keep them from seeing the light of the gospel of the glory of Christ, who is the image of God."[74] This use of the word *world,* is like a great net that our enemy uses to hinder humanity from seeing the truth of the gospel. In a letter to the early church, John warns, "Do not love the world or the things in the world. If any man loves the world, the love of the Father is not in him."[75] This last rendering of the word, *world,* seems plausible, but a system cannot hate the followers of Jesus in a pragmatic sense. An honest evaluation requires that we look for a solution outside of these three options. I would suggest that it is a hybrid of the last two meanings of the word, *world.*

Days before his crucifixion a group of Greeks sought an audience with Jesus. They had come to hear him teach, to listen to his wisdom and philosophy about life. Greek culture elevated man to a godlike status, believing that through deep philosophical discussion the great questions of life could be answered. They believed that man could find purpose and meaning in life through the pursuit of wisdom. Jesus never met with them. Instead, he began speaking to his disciples about his coming crucifixion. He was emphasizing the fact that the only victory over sin and Satan was not to be found in an intellectual pursuit. Man cannot fix his own problems and find a pathway to life.

Therefore, the world hated him because he rejected a man-centered approach to life. When he told Nicodemus that he must be born again Jesus was, in effect, rejecting any hope that mankind can find their way back to God apart from a new birth. Jesus was setting aside human effort as a means of salvation, thus condemning the world. Satan's authority was also judged as unworthy to rescue man from sin. Speaking of his death on the cross he said this, "Now is the judgment of this world; now will the ruler of this world be cast out, And I, when I am lifted up from the earth, will draw all people to myself."[76]

When Jesus walked on the earth, he loved people but rejected this world because it was built on the wrong foundation. It was established by the Devil based on man, not God. The world system we live in is man centered. A system that glorifies the narcissistic tendencies within man is the perfect bait. It is a trap that perfectly matches the drive within mankind brought to bear by his fall into sin. A live shrimp dangling in front of a hungry trout is tempting beyond description. The self-centered nature of man is what keeps him in bondage because the world system perfectly matches his egotistical predisposition.

Subsequently, the foundation that drives this world forward is self-actualization, which is the very thing Jesus rejected in his teaching. Jesus came to destroy the works of the Devil and in doing so has destroyed the kingdom of men. The underpinning of their kingdom is crumbling below their feet, and they rightfully blame the Son of God. Jesus came to reveal the love of God, and the opposite of love is not hate, it is self. It is the men who are tied closely to the world system who are the source of the persecution of Christians. Those who have embraced this world so tightly that they see God, and us, as a threat to their man-centered ideology is the *world* that hates us. The merging of these two elements creates the source of our battle. There are multitudes who don't know Christ, but neither are they too deeply entrenched in this world's system. They are entrapped by it, but they don't fully embrace it. Many of these are sympathetic to the church. It those who love this world, and as a result, hate us because we stand against it.

If we are told that the road between two cities is lined with potholes, then every bump we feel is a reminder we are on the right path. We are marching against the current of this world and should expect a battle. "I have said these things to you, that in me you may have peace. In the world you will have tribulation. But take heart; I have overcome the world."[77] Until we reach the golden shores of eternity, we will face opposition.

༺༻

If the world hates you, know that it has hated
me before it hated you. If you were of this world, the
world would love you as its own; but because you
are not of the world, but I chose you out
of the world, therefore the world hates you.

JOHN 15: 18,19 ESV

CHAPTER 17

The Danger of Indoctrination

Indoctrination. Nasty word. When I hear the term, it congers up visions of small school children marching into a communist classroom to hear propaganda akin to a cheap horror flick. The word carries me down to Guyana where hundreds drank the juice of deception and died at the hands of a mad man. Forced brainwashing is the bread and butter of indoctrination, and it happens slowly, over time. It promises freedom, but that pipe dream is quickly replaced by the pressure to embrace the information presented without questioning it. If troubling inquiries are asked, the follower is made to appear slow or dumb. Raising your hand to ask a question might get you moved to the back of the class and eventually out the door. A dangerous mentality called, *group think,* is adopted and intolerance to free thinking is embraced. Being a member of the *group* stokes a sense of belonging and privilege. Pride is the material of the walls built around the concentration camp of indoctrination.

The goal of those who use indoctrination is to gain like-minded followers who swallow whatever is placed on their highchair. Their hope is to win proselytes, who nod without thinking and digest whatever is being shoveled their way no matter how it smells. Resistance is seen as rebellion, questioning as a form of arrogance. Organizations which use manipulation and pressure do it in the most subtle ways. They appear as smooth and silky as a bedsheet, but underneath, a mattress of thorns awaits those who bite on the spoiled cheddar. We all move to the opposite side of the street when we see them coming. My mother used to hide with my sister in the cellar when she saw those white shirts and black ties walking up to the door.

Unfortunately, indoctrination is not the exclusive domain of the cults. Those who hold orthodox beliefs are also subject to this poisonous approach. Well-meaning followers of Christ can become pushy regarding their beliefs. Unwittingly, they begin to use the tactics of indoctrination. Becoming fully convinced that they have a corner on the truth, they reject all other teachings as harmful and wrong. They further consider it their duty to correct all others and lead them down the right path. Their beliefs are not simply shared in love but forcefully shoved down the throats of their more simple-minded brothers. The result of this tactic is that they repel those who they wish to convince. With this method of force feeding, they cause believers and non-believers alike to run for the hills.

When Jesus spoke with a rich, young ruler, he was talking to a man who wasn't quite ready to hear the truth. Jesus knew this and dealt with him accordingly. He wanted to guide the man into truth, not scalp him. After running to the Savior, the rich young ruler caught his breath and asked him what good thing he must do to inherit eternal life. It was a sincere question, but it contained an obvious flaw. No one receives an inheritance because of something they have done. Inclusion in a will is normally based on being family or friend and is given because someone has died.

Those who love to indoctrinate others would have seen an opportunity to enter a lively debate. They would have salivated to have a chance to engage this wealthy, poor soul. Seeing themselves as guides to the blind they would have surrounded him with their own version of truth. After correcting his question, they would have spun a series of Bible verses together to set a trap and expect him to nod and agree at every point. The young man would have never gotten a word in edgewise.

Rather than become entangled in a pointless debate, Jesus chose to engage the ruler in a discussion. He desired that the man use his brain and think through his position. The rich young ruler produced a list of accomplishments to gain entrance into the celestial city. Jesus countered by asking him to sell all that he had and follow him. The man walked away because he had great riches which he refused to relinquish. The terms Jesus gave him were too steep and the cost too great. The Master did not lay down a long list of doctrines to adhere to, nor did he demand a litmus test of the major tenets of the faith. He told the man to simply abandon all else and follow him.

Now to be clear, there is nothing wrong with holding certain positions if we are respectful of others' beliefs. To attempt to force someone to believe something they are not ready to believe is an act of impertinence. To continue to press our beliefs when the listener obviously has no interest is to violate their sovereign right to believe or not believe what they chose. Indoctrination ruins relationships.

The interesting part of the story of the rich, young ruler is that Jesus did not run after the man to convince him. He respected the decision of this influential man to the point that he allowed him to reject eternal life. Jesus had no desire to indoctrinate him by forcing him to make a decision he was not ready to make. He let the man walk away with the hope that he had planted a seed of truth that would come to fruition one day in the future. When we share the gospel, we should be gentle with those we are attempting to win. Truth is not up for debate, but truth can only be received by those who are ready to believe and that is the work of the Holy Spirit.

We, who know Christ, should share truth. However, we must never seek to force our viewpoints on others. This is not only true concerning evangelism, but also within the fellowship of believers. The attempt to indoctrinate our fellow Christian toward a specific viewpoint is a practice that Jesus refused. Let each man be at peace with what he believes and let the Lord in the end judge our beliefs. If your position is strong, then quietly display the glory of Jesus. You may win your brother to your way of thinking, but you won't do it with a stubborn arrogance that only alienates you from those you are called to love. If your brother is wrong, then let the Lord show him. Our responsibility is not to push our positions upon others. Good men have differed for thousands of years, and yet, have achieved peace together because they rejected the practice of indoctrination. It is our responsibility to love our brother in Christ. No one has ever been won over in a debate, but many a relationship has been injured by the constant pressure of indoctrination. When friendships are left to hang on the thin thread of opinions, they cease to exist. Indoctrination is a nasty word and an ugly practice. Let those who name the name of Christ resist and reject it at every point.

Who are you to pass judgment on the servant of another? It is before his own master that he stands or falls. And he will be upheld, for the Lord is able to make him stand.

ROMANS 15:4 ESV

CHAPTER 18

A Pigeon Named Joseph

T he following is a parable about a pigeon named Joseph, who, through his fowl behavior, destroyed a community of his fellow pigeons.

Once upon a time there was a brightly colored pigeon named Joseph, who was part of a community called Three Streams. His colorful coat stood out in contrast to the ordinary feathers of his fellow birds in the village, and this is where the trouble began. Joseph viewed himself as superior to the common looking fowl in town and often thought to himself how fortunate they were to have him there. He also considered his opinions and oratory skills a level above those of his comrades although he was careful to conceal that fact. The appearance of humility was key to his deception, and Joseph played the part well. Over time, Joseph became extremely proud of his humility. And then, one sunny Sunday morning, as Joseph was speaking on a particular point of view in the city square, he noticed the crowd before him was frowning. Perhaps, he thought, the breakfast buffet that morning had included something that did not agree with them. Joseph continued to press his point even though he was facing a group of pigeons who were becoming increasingly antagonistic toward his address. Line upon line, precept upon precept, he persevered to the very end. Many of the birds looked at things differently than Joseph, and this offended him greatly.

After Joseph's oration in the city square, counsels were called, and meetings were scheduled. Even a town gathering was held to try to find middle ground regarding Joseph's strange new line of thought, but no reasonable consensus was reached. The brightly colored pigeon of Three Streams stomped about with his feathers all in a ruffle until he had stirred everyone into a tizzy. The rest of the birds, though, held their ground.

Angry with the village of Three Streams, Joseph packed his things, gathered his little family under his wing, and stormed away. He could've chosen to leave amicably, but he allowed his temper to fog his judgement. When members of his old community would see him on the street, he would simply smile and walk away without saying a word. An undeniable cloud of resentment hung over Joseph's head that he refused to acknowledge. An older, wiser pigeon tried to counsel Joseph, but he told the elder that all was well and that he harbored no animosity toward those who still lived in Three Streams. The old pigeon knew better.

With great opinions and grand ideas, Joseph decided to establish a new community on a frozen pond to the north of Three Streams in a place called Shallow Well. However, this new venture was doomed to fail. No matter how much he smiled his beaky smile and pushed on with his fresh start, his bad spirit remained firmly intact. Joseph was at risk of not only destroying himself but all the pigeons who followed him to Shallow Well.

For a while, all seemed well in the tiny village on the frozen pond until one very sad day. Joseph had been spending time stomping around in a muddy swamp at the edge of town to relieve his burdened spirit over what had happened in Three Streams. Joseph did not want anyone to know about his private fits of anger, but his muddy feet began to burn into the icy surface of the pond. The brightly colored pigeon ignored the mess that the mud was making, hoping that in time all would be washed away. Then one day, as Joseph was making a great speech and displaying his brightly colored feathers, the ice below his feet cracked, and the entire community of pigeons sank into the frozen pond never to be heard of again.

In the end, it was all a great mess, causing pigeon communities from all over the land to shake their heads and speak ill of the communities of Three Streams and Shallow Well. The poison of what had happened in those two pigeon communities was even discussed at length among other animal groups, but mainly the weasel population. Three Streams, for their part of the debacle, limped on for years never achieving anything greater than their own selfish expectations.

There are three lessons to be learned from our friend with the brightly colored feathers.

First, if your feathers are brighter than those of your fellow pigeons resist the temptation to think you are something special. If God has blessed you with certain advantages such as talent, wealth, or even good looks, pay no attention to it. No one really cares. You are no better than the plain colored pigeons. In the end, your feathers will fade, and your beak will droop. Consider the possibility that God has gifted you for the purpose of serving your fellow birds. Of the six things that the Lord hates, a proud look is the first on the list.[78]

Secondly, be open to the counsel of trusted friends. Amid volatile situations, when emotions run high, it impossible to be completely objective. Who better than a friend who loves you to show you your dark side? "Iron sharpens iron, and one man sharpens another."[79] A good friend is like a mirror on a car that shows you your blind spot. When things within a community of pigeons gets messy, there are no innocent parties. Everyone on the ball diamond threw punches; don't deny the swings you threw in the fray. The mud on your fellow bird's feather was thrown by someone. Mark Twain once said, "Everyone is a moon and has a dark side which he never shows to anyone."[80]

Lastly, if you begin something new with anger and bitterness toward something or someone in your past, your new endeavors will fail in time. A new marriage, a new job, and especially a new church will fold like a deck of cards under the weight of the anger burning in your soul. To deny its presence is a game for fools. The pressure cooker of such emotions will come to the top and explode in your face. King David saw the futility of restraining the beast within him. "I said, I will take heed to my ways, that I sin not with my tongue: I will keep my mouth with a bridal, while the wicked is before me. I was done with silence, I held my peace, even from good; and my sorrow was stirred. My heart was hot within me, while I was musing the fire burned: then spake I with my tongue. LORD, make me to know mine end, and the measure of my days, what it is; that I may know how frail I am."[81] David was not only honest concerning what was in his heart, he was also humble before the Lord in the confession of his anger. His fury led him to the realization of his own frailty.

Do not deny the anger and bitterness within, it will only fester. Resentment is a miserable tenant who needs to be evicted. "See to it that no one fails to obtain the grace of God; that no root of bitterness springs up and causes trouble, and by it many become defiled."[82] Roots must be completely pulled out of the ground, or they will sprout again. The poison ivy of bitterness will give painful rashes in all who come near it.

The remedy is as clear as a rainbow after a summer storm. Apart from Jesus Christ, there is no victory over resentment and bitterness. Acknowledge the anger and thank God for his forgiveness. Forgive yourself for the harm and damage you have done. Go back to the place of hurt and ask for forgiveness. Reconcile with your fellow pigeons if possible. As much as is possible in you, be at peace with all birds. God will not bless a new path otherwise. You will know you have victory when you can walk down the same side of the street as the one you have offended and have perfect peace. You can speak their name with ease. Most importantly, they no longer occupy space in your mind, cluttering your thoughts and heart with poison. They may even become your friend again.

I love telling stories, so I tend to look at life like chapters in a book. New chapters are marked by the events of our lives that alter us. If the new chapter you are attempting to write is marred by the ugliness of the last, it will not end well. Turn the pages back and make things right before going forward. "Repay no one evil for evil but give thought to do what is honorable in the sight of all. If possible, so far as it depends on you, live peaceably with all."[83] There is a name for stories that follow the path of bitterness to the end. They are called tragedies. God desires for us a happy ending.

᎒᎒᎒

If possible, so far as it depends on you, live peaceably with all.

ROMANS 12:18 ESV

CHAPTER 19

Climate Change

Our planet is heating up. Any fair and honest observer must admit that this spinning globe is on a direct path to a fiery inferno. The nightly news trumpets, with story after story, undeniable evidence of a dismal future. If climate change will be the end of us all, how shall we stop it? We shouldn't. In fact, what we desperately need *is* climate change. Yes, you read that correctly; we must experience a dramatic climate change to survive as a human race. An alteration in our present environment is the only thing which will pull us out of this tailspin and set us on solid ground. The need is so great for climate change that only a world-shaking transformation for the entire globe will suffice. Not only are we on the right path for this change, but its acceleration is also abundantly evident. Why is the need so great?

Today, believers see the atmosphere of our world culture is so poisoned with hate and fraught with sickness and discouragement that our only hope is for the present world order to be scrapped. In the past, we have pulled ourselves out of terrible *world-ending* situations, but this present dilemma cries out for a new beginning. We need a *new* world order. This fresh beginning requires a new foundation unlike any we have known before in human experience. The only thing that will change the climate of our world this dramatically, and the change that is clearly on the near horizon, is the return of Jesus Christ. His appearance in the clouds of glory will instantly change our current climate forever. The true, righteous King is our only hope. Hallelujah!

Unfortunately, his arrival will not be met with applause and fanfare. "Then will appear in heaven the sign of the Son of Man, and then all the tribes of the earth will mourn, and they will see the Son of Man coming on the clouds of heaven with power and great glory."[84] It is a sad commentary that men have resisted their need of God ever since their exit from the Garden of Eden. The sons of Adam just need a little more time to get it right, they think. The next generation will no doubt find the answers to hatred and violence. A new crop of more intelligent homo sapiens will eradicate drug abuse and domestic violence. The age of Aquarius is upon us as love and peace will reign. Scientists work feverishly to create a pill that will cause the masses to fall in line and no longer rebel against authority. Technology has exploded on the scene with the promise of curing the rat race of mankind. However, human government is useless without self-governing, and that has failed for centuries. John Adams stated, "Public virtue cannot exist in a Nation without private Virtue, and public Virtue is the only Foundation of Republics."[85] Each new change in our political landscape eventually brings the same old song and dance of greater and greater heartache and death upon the nations.

During the time of Noah humanity had spiraled downhill at an alarming rate. The society of his day had degenerated to the point of no return. "The LORD saw that the wickedness of man was great in the earth, and that every intention of the thoughts of his heart was only evil continually."[86]

Clearly, God had to step in and change the climate, or mankind would have destroyed itself. They ate, drank, and were living in a condition that can only be described as godless. Even though they knew there was a Creator, they had so eradicated him from their minds that they walked with a fearless abandonment into every sort of sin and depravity. When they came across Noah out in the wilderness building a massive ship, it became a source of great entertainment and intense conversation. *Foolish Noah*, they no doubt called him. His building project gave their sad lives something to talk about, and to laugh at, at least until the heavens opened and the rain came. The flood was sent to cleanse the earth so that God could begin anew. The Lord brought the first climate change with the flood, and he would do it again when Israel entered the Promise Land.

At the time of the patriarch Abraham, Canaan was home to one of the most corrupt cultures this earth has ever known. Idol worship, child sacrifice, and perverse immorality were just some of the common practices in the land that one day would bear the name of Israel. Sodom and Gomorrah bore the judgement of God by being destroyed with fire and brimstone, and that was hundreds of years before the Jewish nation entered the land to take possession of it. The evolution of evil that occurred in those years is unimaginable. When the promise of the land was given to Abraham, the Lord made an interesting statement. He stated that the sin of the Amorites was not yet full. God, before bringing judgement, was waiting to see if the people who occupied Canaan land would repent. Before bringing climate change in Canaan, he graciously waited for the people to change it themselves. They didn't, and so, God brought judgment through Joshua's invasion. The Jews were told to enter the land and wipe out an entire culture. The only way to bring in the climate change of righteousness is to eradicate the deadly poison of sin and evil. When Jesus returns, the climate of humanity will be changed forever.

There is nothing so constant as change. The clouds rolling over our heads today will be replaced by a new set of circumstances completely different from the day before. The months flow naturally into years, and before we know it, life has expired, and we stand before our Maker. Having said all that, these last days go down as some of the worst in history. Civil unrest, political upheaval, a world-wide pandemic, and now, a war that threatens our very existence, has descended upon us with little warning. Any one of these would be enough to send a stress fraction throughout our world, but all of these at once have threatened to open a cavernous divide, pulling us all into the abyss of despondency. A sense of hopelessness has settled over our world, and no amount of positive rhetoric or empty promises of better days will help stem the tide of sadness and misery we all feel.

Only Jesus can bring the climate change this world is crying out for but unable to achieve. He alone can bring peace and healing to a fractured world. As a side benefit of his return, he will also institute the new green deal. Our planet will thrive again as the polluted oceans are instantly cleaned and the woodlands are restored to their original glory. Air pollution will be eradicated, and we will return to a planet much like the Garden of Eden.

Climate change is exactly what we need, but unlike the warning of a catastrophe that would destroy us, this sudden altercation of our present toxic climate is exactly what we need. Jesus will bring a change to the climate of our world instantly in the hearts and minds of people. The Prince of Peace will arrive with healing in his wings. The new green deal that Jesus will bring will cost us nothing, but it will be priceless to see and experience. Are you ready for zero toxic emissions from the evil that is now growing? Our world is no doubt heating up, and I am excited for its future.

⌒◯◯◯◯◯◯⌒

I will lift up mine eyes unto the hills, from whence cometh my help. My help cometh from the Lord, which made heaven and earth.

PSALM 121:1,2 KJV

CHAPTER 20

Tall Tales

The tales of Paul Bunyan and Babe, the Big Blue Ox, were some of my favorites as a child. I would laugh at the five storks it took to carry Bunyan as a baby. The river he drank to satisfy his unquenchable thirst captivated my imagination. I wondered if it were true that by simply dropping his axe Paul Bunyan had created the Grand Canyon. The stories of this giant man in our ordinary world were born, not with ink and paper, but in logging camps from Maine to Oregon. Lonely tree cutters sat around campfires and cabin stoves attempting to outdo one another with tales of Paul Bunyan's amazing deeds.

Will H. Dilg relates some of the stories told in the DeKalb Daily Chronicle in 1925, "Bunyan had an expert crew. There were the famous Seven Axemen, who cut down whole forests in a day by tying axe heads to ropes and advancing through the forest swinging them in great circles. And there was his expert cook, Ole, who carved his own niche in the hall of fame when he came to the rescue on the occasion of the Blue Ox dumping all of the winter's supply of beans into Round Pond. Ole took one look and then built a fire under the pond, making bean soup of the whole thing."[87]

While growing up in the hills of upstate New York, I had a childhood friend who told tall tales. They usually involved spectacular stories of his father's exploits. I would listen patiently to his dad's amazing feats and try not to let on that I knew the fictional accounts dwelt more in my friend's mind than reality. His father was gone much of the time as a trucker, and perhaps it was a way for my friend to feel close to him. He loved his dad, and looking back, it was sweet. However, what is quaint in a little boy, and fascinating to read in a fictional story, is repulsive in any other realm. Tall tales should be left to storytellers who invent fun characters for imaginative minds. In the real world we want truth. We want to be told the facts, especially from those in authority, and when we are not, we lose confidence in them. People and institutions lose our trust. We are at a point in our culture where it is becoming increasingly difficult to believe anyone in authority, and that is a sad reality.

My grandson was peering through a glass of cocktail juice the other morning and observed that everything on the breakfast table looked red. Everyone is looking through a different glass of juice these days, and we are being told a dozen different accounts of the same event. Creating false narratives to spin an event is a dangerous game. Tomorrow's headlines are crafted before the dust settles. By doing this, they are attempting to manipulate the outcome and gain favorable public opinion. People are presumed guilty before the jury has had time to warm their chairs.

It is becoming apparent to most of us that the only place we can turn to find truth is God's word, and perhaps, that has always been true. After all, false narratives are nothing new. People have been retelling events to their own fancy since the days of Adam and Eve. When God confronted the first couple concerning their sin, they both spun the story to their own liking. Ignoring the facts on the ground, Eve blamed the serpent, Adam blamed the woman, and the snake snickered in the bushes. The Father of lies has been roaming this earth for thousands of years, whispering in ears, and then laughing in the shadows. The truth these days is harder to find than a thin needle in a thousand haystacks. Men cannot be relied on to pull us out of the tailspin we are now experiencing. Is there no place to anchor our souls to the rock solid of truth?

When Moses was leading over a million thirsty Jews through the wilderness, he came to the rock of Horeb. The people had been complaining to Moses concerning the lack of water and were at the point of stoning him. The same man who had led them out of bondage and through the Red Sea was now in danger of losing his life. The Lord told Moses to take the same staff he had used to split the Red Sea and hit the rock. After collecting the elders of Israel, he did so, and water came pouring out of the rock. The need of the moment was met, and catastrophe was averted. Did the Israelites learn their lesson? No, before long they would be complaining about the lack of meat. The daily manna had grown boring to them, and they desired meat. Like those ancient wilderness wanderers, we are slow to trust God's word. We tend to look for encouragement in all the wrong places. God did provide for them meat to eat, and he still does so today.

The Bible is our only hope to navigate these troubled times. The truths shared within Scripture are eternal and reliable because they speak of One who can be counted on to rescue us. "God is our refuge and strength, a very present help in trouble."[88] "Give us help from trouble, for the help of man is useless," David cried out.[89] Truer words have never been spoken. If you have ever been left waiting at the train station of encouragement from others, you understand that man's help is a dollar short and a day late. In Hebrews. the writer encourages his readers by saying, "The Lord is my helper; I will not fear; what can man do to me?" He goes on to write, "Keep your life free from love of money, and be content with what you have, for he has said, "I will never leave you nor forsake you."[90]

The Bible is the hook I'm hanging my hat on these days. In fact, I'm hanging my coat, my pants, my shirt, and even my skivvies on what the Bible teaches. Let's choose to hang everything on the peg of biblical truth. Faith is born and nourished by truth, and the only truth I'm witnessing these days is between the leather cover of my Bible. The evening news will only depress you; shut it off and feed on the Bread of Life.

〇⟭⟭⟭〇

Give us help from trouble, for the help of man is useless.

PSALMS 60:11 ESV

CHAPTER 21

Kingdom in a Cave

The Allegory of the Cave is a story written by the Greek philosopher, Plato. It is a tale about a group of people who were chained to the wall of a cavern their entire lives. While looking at the walls of the cave, they observed shadows from the world above, to which they gave names. These images, though mere silhouettes, became their reality. The cave was all they knew from childhood, as life above ground did not exist in their minds. Escape from the cave was difficult, and yet, once achieved did not guarantee true freedom for the fugitive. A return to the underground grotto was always a danger once true images were observed and rejected as false. To embrace the familiar, even though it is but shadows, dooms man in the cave of ignorance forever.

Plato's goal was to reveal the importance of education in removing our shadowy concepts of life. Education, in Plato's mind, was the means to bridge the gap when bringing a child into the true reality of adulthood. To the Greek philosopher, knowledge was the key to life and meaning. As helpful as knowledge is, it does not bring us ultimately to the true meaning of why we are here on earth. There is a different bridge needed, and so, I would like to use Plato's allegory in the spiritual realm. We have all been born in the spiritual darkness of a cave, of which, there is no escape. We simply cannot find our way to the surface by ourselves. Our only hope is to be rescued.

The defining feature of the cave is that we are kept in the shadows of a dark and damp existence. Our entire perspective is skewed by our inability to see things clearly. We draw conclusions and make decisions based on cloudy lenses. To make matters worse, we rely on fellow cave dwellers to teach and guide us into deeper and darker passages of hopelessness. The rocky corridors begin to close in on us, and yet, we move steadily forward. Others promise us a way out of the cave only to lead to dead ends and despair.

Within this cavern of shadows, random events and tragic occurrences become the stinging reality of our time here on earth. We are all born into the kingdom of men, and the cave is all we know. Random calamity and heartache strike us all when we least expect it. Constant and unfolding misfortune, producing tragedy, is our common experience. As hard as we fight to structure life and produce a desired end, this kingdom of the cave repeatedly punches us in the gut. We fight and claw for our place in the cave, all the while death looms over us like a dark cloud. The shadows on the wall remind us that there is a light somewhere above, but we are strangely satisfied to watch the pale movements in the rocks. We are all miners in Plato's story and have clung to the falsehood that we can never be free. Striving to defeat the beast of death and disaster, we waste our days plotting our next move. The rumbling in the cave tells us that someday it will collapse on us. We know we will die someday; we just don't want it to be today.

Compared to the reality of the spiritual life, this earth-bound existence is shadowy at best. Paul, in writing to the Corinthians, described it like this, "For now, we see in a mirror dimly, but then face to face. Now I know in part; then I shall know fully, even as I have been fully known."[91] C.S. Lewis, in his seventh book in the series, *The Chronicles of Narnia*, concludes with a conversation between Asian and Lucy concerning death. Asian tells her, "Your father and mother and all of you are- as you used to call it in the Shadowlands- dead. The term is over: the holidays have begun. The dream is ended: this is the morning."[92] What appears to be reality in the cave, is nothing more than the echoes of a truer drum beat in the realm of the spiritual life.

It is not until Christ enters our lives that these shadowy concepts of reality begin to lift. We imagine death to be our common lot until Jesus enters the equation and offers life eternal. The light that we suspected to be above us bursts into full glory, and the shadows flee giving way to the true reality of the heavenly life. The light is at once immediate and progressive in nature. We were men without hope until the glorious offer of Christ arrived in the gentle voice, "Come unto me."[93] One of the early hymns of the church is quoted in the book of Ephesians, "For anything that becomes visible is light. Therefore, it says, 'Awake, O sleeper, and arise from the dead, and Christ will shine on you."[94] Without Jesus this life is but a sleep, and the sinner is encouraged to arise from the deadness of the cave. The apostle Paul, in his defense to the violent mob in Jerusalem, described his conversion on the road to Damascus. "As I was on my way and drew near to Damascus, about noon a great light from Heaven suddenly shone around me."[95] He told King Agrippa years later that he was not disobedient to the heavenly vision. None of us know we are in the dark until the light arrives through the work of the Holy Spirit.

When a man emerges from a cave, there are a few moments that he hides his eyes from the sun. His vision is so adjusted to the darkness of the cave, that it takes some time to allow his sight to enjoy full light. However, once he acclimates to his new world, he is amazed at the life swirling all around him. The smudge of living in the cave is washed clean by the light now streaming into his soul. He begins to realize his new freedom, and when he does, all the attraction of the cave will hold no interest for him. The man set free by Christ walks with a confidence he never knew before. He wonders why he didn't come out into the light sooner. To his astonishment, those who remain in the cave rarely listen to his new discovery. Such is the case for the new Christian.

The New Testament teaches that we have been delivered from the power of darkness. Our new kingdom is one of light, freedom, and glory. We have been set free from guilt and shame. The power of sin, that once held us in its deadly grip, is forever broken. Likewise, we are no longer to think in terms of death. We no longer fear our mortality but see it as a glorious entrance into Heaven. Paul once wrote, "I desire to depart and be with Christ."[96] In his book, *A Tale of Two Cities*, Charles Dickens notes, "It is a far, far, better thing that I do than I have ever done, it is a far, far, better rest that I go to than I have ever known."[97] For those who have received Christ, the shadows of the cave are no longer our dwelling place. Eternity awaits our arrival.

C. S. Lewis finishes his adventures in Narnia with this closing observation, "All their life in this world and all their adventures in Narnia had only been the cover and the title page: now at last they were beginning Chapter One of the Great Story which no one on earth has read: which goes on forever: in which every chapter is better than the one before."[98] Enjoy the sunlight today.

⌒൜൜⌒

For to me to live is Christ, and to die is gain.

PHILIPPIANS 1:21 ESV

CHAPTER 22

The Sound of Many Waters

Since the beginning of time, oceans have captivated our imagination. From the Pacific down around Cape Horn back up to the Atlantic, great bodies of water have defined our continents. The yet unexplored regions of the seas still charm the adventurer in us all. Having spent a few years sailing on the deep blue sea, I have always been fascinated by its grandeur. The magnificence of the ocean is as astounding as its size is enormous. And yet, with all its roaring splendor and glory, it finds its end on a soft beach next to a child building a sandcastle. Its saltiness stings our eyes and heals our wounds, and its rhythm causes us to dream of deserted islands filled with strange creatures. The stories of pirates who plunder for treasures of gold and bottles filled with messages washing up on distant shores fixate our minds. After casting a dim eye toward land lovers, sailors have for centuries boarded ships and pulled up anchors. Heading out to sea, they embraced the salty mist and the constant swell of deep waters. Alongside our fascination with the oceans, the Bible has much to say concerning these great bodies of water.

In the book of Isaiah, the prophet wrote, "Ah, the thunder of many peoples; they thunder like the thundering of the sea! Ah, the roar of nations; they roar like the roaring of mighty waters! The nations roar like the roaring of many waters…,"[99] Oswald Chambers said this, "the roaring of the seas, the roaring of their waves, and the tumult of the people, and those words might well put us onto the right track for the meaning of our Lord's words, the roaring of the sea refers to the nations."[100] Consider the similarities seas have with humanity.

Looking out over the great waters of the earth, we see instability. Oceans are easily whipped into a frenzy by an angry wind. As mighty as they appear, seas are at the mercy of the storms that rage just above their surface. At one point the oceans appear smooth as glass, and then, moments later, become roaring torrents able to sink ships. In a similar way, men are unstable and erratic, being manipulated by elements beyond their control. External pressures mount quickly among world leaders causing them to change course and wreak havoc on the world. Innocent voyagers are at the mercy of these world leaders. The raging tempest of volatile nations has marked the history of our world leaving the nation's stability at the mercy of the next crashing wave. Filled with evil, Hitler marched across Europe causing death, and destruction. Moa Tse Tung and Joseph Stalin were responsible for killing more than 65 million people in their reigns of terror.

Furthermore, throughout the ages, poets, song writers, and authors have compared the oceans to mankind. Oceans are deep bodies of water with most of their activity hidden from view. With their strong undercurrents, they sway ships and guide marine life. The great kingdoms of this world have always operated in secret leaving us woefully ignorant of their dark processes. In hidden bunkers, deep underground, strong currents of secret societies are formed for the purpose of satisfying their insatiable lust for power and wealth. Like icebergs floating past unsuspecting ships, we see very little of their danger until it is too late. The puppet governments they install are for the purpose of concealing their true intent. As in the vision of Daniel, these hideous beasts finally emerge and reveal themselves in their true form.

Finally, the oceans are only navigated by looking into the heavens. Sailors for centuries have reached their destinations or been lost at sea by their ability to read the stars. Too many cloud-filled nights will cause ships to veer off course and sailors to lose their lives. God placed the stars in the heavens to remind us of his faithfulness. Unlike the instability of unpredictable waters, the stars in heaven remain constant and can be depended upon to give guidance. Mankind is doomed apart from the North Star.

In the Scriptures, the seas are also symbolic of humanity. In one of the great visions in the book of Daniel, four hideous beasts are seen rising out of a great sea after it had been stirred up by the winds of heaven.[101] These beasts prophesy four world empires that would rise and fall before the second coming of the Son of God. Men view these mighty kingdoms with awe while God sees them as dreadful creatures. Men are impressed by empires built by men; God is repulsed by man's effort to supplant his rule and reign. From this turbulent sea of humanity men would emerge who would unsuccessfully try to rule the world. These kingdoms were the Babylonians, the Persians, the Greeks, and the Romans. Their destiny and boundaries were set by God. All of them were crushed in preparation for the Lord's return to this earth. Throughout the biblical narrative, bodies of water represented mankind.

When the children of Israel left Egypt, they were chased to the edges of the Red Sea by the Egyptian army. What appeared to be a hopeless situation turned into a great miracle of deliverance as God split the waters. In parting the Red Sea, God was separating his people from all other nations. The Red Sea experience illustrated God's ability to set apart a people for his own glory. The Egyptian's army drowned in those same waters foreshadowing his judgment on humanity for their treatment of the people of God.

When Jonah refused to preach to the people of Nineveh, he was cast into the sea. His desire to exclusively preach to the Jewish nation earned him a ride inside a great fish. Spending a few days in the belly of the whale gave Jonah time to reconsider his bigotry against a nation not his own. After conducting the first amphibious landing, he marched begrudgingly up to Nineveh preaching doom and gloom. The great city repented, and Jonah marched away angry. God had cast him into the sea of humanity, but he still failed to learn his lesson. How patient is the Lord with all of us!

During the Lord's time on this earth, he walked on the sea of Galilee and commanded the waves to be calmed when storms arose. In these two miracles he displayed his authority, not only over the forces of nature, but also over humanity itself. When Jesus first called Peter, he invited him to fish for men. After his resurrection, he met his disciples on the shores of the Sea of Galilee. Peter, once again, dragged fish out of the lake to remind him of his commission to fish in the sea of humanity.

The apostle John was given a revelation of the glorified Christ on the island of Patmos. Surrounded by the Mediterranean Sea, it was a perfect setting for God to reveal his plan for humanity. John described the voice of Jesus as the sound of many waters. As Heaven had invaded the shoreline of humanity in the person of Jesus Christ, so now John heard his voice as mighty waters. When Jesus returns to this earth, all men will hear his voice. Humanity will not be able to ignore it any longer. Being taken up into Heaven, John saw the throne of God surrounded by twenty-four elders and four beasts. Lightning and thunder proceeded from the throne. He saw a sea of glass, clear as crystal amid the throne. Humanity, finally at peace, was pictured at the feet of God's throne. No waves of rebellion or even ripples of discord now existed because the Lord sat in authority over mankind.

The greatest dreams and aspirations of humanity are nothing compared to what God is preparing for those who love him. When Jesus returns, men will live together in perfect harmony. The world will enter a period of peace where Christ will rule on this earth for a thousand years. After this, sin will be judged, and man will enter an eternal state of bliss wherein there is no more sea. The threat of men, rising in rebellion, will end.

When John the apostle finally reaches the last chapter of the Revelation, he notices a river of life flowing out from the throne. The sea has been replaced with the nourishing flow of the river of life. The instability of the seas will be replaced with an eternal fountain of life. That river is available right now to all who believe in Jesus Christ. Today, come to the fountain that never runs dry.

∞

...and his voice was like the roar of many waters.

REVELATION 1:15 ESV

CHAPTER 23

Finished

Christianity is a finished work. This truth has huge implications for the child of God regarding his peace and growth. When Jesus died on the cross, he paid for our sins in full and then took us with him into the grave. When he came out of that grave, three days later, we came with him having received new life. In our statement of baptism we recite, "Buried in death with Christ, raised in newness of life." According to Paul, the death, burial, and resurrection of Christ is the core of the gospel.[102] Everything begins and ends with the passion narrative of Jesus and how it has impacted those who follow him. Christian psychology, best understood, is not the study of the Christian, it is an understanding of the life of Jesus within a believer. It is Christ in you, the hope of glory.[103]

Based on that fact alone, God doesn't need our help with any part of our Christian experience. All we need for growth and maturity was given to us when we were born again. As the design of a plant is in the seed, so our entire spiritual life was planted in us when we became his followers. Growth is a matter of faith and rest in what God has accomplished at the cross of Christ. "For we walk by faith, not by sight."[104] We do not add to our sanctification by effort. Our striving in the realm of self-discipline only hinders his work in us. Christian growth is not a collaborative effort; God alone produces the fruit as we abide in the vine.[105] This truth is clearly seen in the natural world.

At the start of each new day, we are greeted with birds singing sweetly, and trees swaying in the breeze. Long before we arrived on the scene, God has been taking care of his creation. The rain that blesses the grass, and the lightning that cleans the air are all his ideas. The sun warms our faces and causes crops to grow. Each evening he lays the day to rest in grand panoramic gestures quite apart from our advice or input. I have never been awakened by the Lord at five o'clock in the morning for the purpose of helping him with the sunrise. He has been accomplishing these amazing feats without our help, and he will continue when our physical bodies lie cold in the grave. God does not need our help with anything!

Now, what is true of the created order is equally true of God's plan for our lives. This principle of the divine prerogative has always been in operation. Adam and Eve were created on the sixth day of creation signifying an important truth. All creation was finished before they received their first breath from God. Adam's opinion never entered into the design of Paradise. Man was created and then told to join God in a day of rest. Mankind's first full day in the Garden was designed by the Creator to be a day of rest. Our first day entering the glory of Heaven will include an offer from an eternal fountain ever flowing and freely given.

At the end of the book of Revelation, John closes with an invitation to come and take of the water of life. The Spirit and the Bride begin the bidding as they simply say, *Come*. Next, the one who hears and the one who is thirsty are invited to the water. Finally, those who desire, are encouraged to come, and drink. These invitations aren't prefaced with anything other than the fact that the offer has been made, and the one who comes must be dry and desperate. The prophet Isaiah encouraged the people to come and buy wine and milk without price.[106] According to Isaiah, the recipients of the blessings of God are to claim them because they are penniless and hungry. The spiritual life is a gift to be received, not something that we earn. If we reach for our wallet, grace is derailed. Paul did not frustrate the grace of God by working to achieve a level of spirituality. He went so far as to say that if righteousness came by human effort, then Christ's death was useless.[107] When a church or religion gives you a list of things to do to gain spiritual ground, run for the hills.

Rather than our own efforts, the Lord's desire is that we receive as a gift all that we need for our blessing and life from him. We were created to draw life from God. Our lives were always meant to be marked by a restful peace, even in our labor. The hurried, frazzled life is a result of rejecting the rest God offers. Jesus said that if we are burdened with life that we should come to him to find rest. We look for peace down a thousand rabbit holes, and we crawl out of those holes empty-handed and frustrated. Only Christ can satisfy the longing of the human heart. He promised that his yoke was easy and his burden light. Rest for the soul comes as a result of learning from him.[108] However, this type of rest is not inactivity or laziness. God's rest involves relying on him for the strength to live life with vigor.

In Paul's letter to his young protégé, Timothy, he commanded him to stir up the gift of God that was within him. "For this reason, I remind you to fan into flame the gift of God, which is in you through the laying on of my hands."[109] Timothy is not encouraged to seek something new but to fan the fire that already existed within him. This was accomplished, according to Paul, by believing that God had already given Timothy the spirit of fearlessness, power, love, and a sound mind. The words, *stir up*, come from the Greek word *diegeiro*, and it means to wake fully, to arouse. The command implies that it was something Timothy had neglected. He was not told to start a fire; he was reminded of the fire that was present within him, and all it needed was his attention. He was admonished to wake up to the truth that Christ dwelt within him.

For some reason, Timothy had allowed the fire to burn down, and he was experiencing fear. The remedy was not to pull himself up by his bootstraps or to dig deep for an untapped reservoir of courage within himself. The answer was to give the oxygen of faith to the bed of coals ready to flare up. What did the apostle mean by fanning the flame of the gift of God?

When we rise in the morning, we awake to the reality of our surroundings. We have left the dreams of the night for the reality of the day. Timothy was commanded to look, by faith, to the reality of the gift already present within him. The gift of God Paul was referring to was God himself. It was not a gift *from* God that was in view, neither was it a variety of gifts. The *gift* was none other than God himself. Paul does not present to Timothy a smorgasbord of individual blessings to fill his plate. It is the Lord who possesses courage, power, love, and mental stability in infinite measure, and since Timothy's life was buried in Christ, those same attributes were his to claim. He just needed to believe to receive what he already possessed.

In Christ, we have all that we need for ministry and life. God's life in us is more than sufficient for our daily walk through this world. Timothy did not need to ask for a victory he already possessed. He did not need to trudge on through the thick of ministry relying on his own strength. Since Christ dwells within, there is no place for burn out or rust out for the Christian. Fear is unnatural for those who are more than conquerors in Christ. Timothy was simply to trust Jesus through the channel of a sincere faith to walk in victory. We are to rely in that same truth. Christ is the fire within us, and all that is required for it to burn brightly is the fan of faith.

Are you struggling as a believer to live the Christian life? Fight no longer; the battle was won long ago on the cross of Christ. The work is all his; not ours. His life was meant to be the source of our own daily existence. What a Savior! Hallelujah!

I do not nullify the grace of God, for if righteousness were through the law, then Christ died for no purpose.

GALATIANS 2:21 ESV

CHAPTER 24

Unshakable

By most acceptable standards, I consider myself a reasonably intelligent fellow, but I am having a bit of difficulty understanding a recent cultural phenomenon. I am struggling to wrap my brain around the phrase, "cancel culture." What exactly does that mean? The best I can understand, if I say or do something that someone, somewhere in a faraway enclave of a virtual community does not agree with, I can be cancelled. Cancelled from what? Who has the power to perform this dastardly deed and why should I care? If I am canceled, can I be uncanceled? The questions are endless. Am I canceled in the same way you would cancel a television series with poor ratings or a magazine you no longer want? If I am canceled, can I be reinstated by obeying whatever rules they have placed upon me? Maybe I've been cancelled, and I don't even know it. Perhaps I should crawl back in bed and cancel all my appointments and scrap my daily planner. I was excited about an upcoming project, but if I've been canceled, what's the use of completing it? Let's take a different look at this term and hopefully gain a higher perspective from Scripture. Perhaps, we will discover that the *cancel* culture's debilitating nature is not so destructive after all.

Regardless, the idea of canceling people has been around since the beginning of time with little success to show for its efforts. In fact, people usually became louder after being dipped in wax and lit on fire. Cain attempted to cancel Abel by killing him, but his blood still speaks today as a symbol of a righteous man's offering to God. The world mocked Noah when he built an ark on dry ground, but their efforts to marginalize him failed, and everyone except his family drowned in a flood. Pharoah tried to wipe out the Jewish people by chasing them across the desert, and his army died in the Red Sea. Paul thought he had silenced Stephen by orchestrating his stoning, but the young rabbi couldn't get the image of Stephen's death out of his mind. The Romans attempted to silence the apostle John by throwing him in a vat of boiling oil, but he survived with no injury. Seeing they could not kill him, they exiled him to the island of Patmos, and God responded by giving him the greatest revelation known to man. When the world tries to cancel the voice of God's people, they only set our platform on a higher plain. It is like stepping on a mother spider only to have its babies scatter everywhere. The stories are endless.

For instance, Elijah called down fire from the sky moments after the prophets of Baal attempted to silence him. Herod ran a sword through the belly of James, and that night an angel opened the prison for Peter so he could preach in the Temple the next day. The Greeks threw Paul and Silas in a jail cell, and as they sang praises to God, a Philippian jailer got a taste of the power of God.

Before the Lord's crucifixion, Peter was at the lowest point in his life. Confident that he would stand with Jesus in the moment of his Lord's greatest trial, he had folded like a cheap suit. By attempting to separate a man from his head, he had resorted to anger in the Garden. Soon after, he stood on a cold porch warming his hands with the men who had arrested Jesus. Kicking a rooster out of his way, Peter tried to leave but was stopped abruptly at the gate by a young servant girl. He blocked his ears from the question he knew she would ask, "You are one of his, aren't you?" Peter felt cancelled out by his own failure. God was not done with Peter, nor will he ever be with you.

The writer to the Hebrews stated this, "Therefore let us be grateful for receiving a kingdom that cannot be shaken, and thus let us offer to God acceptable worship with reverence and awe."[110] Notice the verse does not say that we *have* received the kingdom, neither does it say that we *will* receive the kingdom at some future time. The verse declares that we are, at this present time, receiving the kingdom of God. In contrast to a world that threatens to cancel us, God encourages us to be grateful because we are in the process of receiving a kingdom that will never be canceled, because it is unshakable. Soon, the mouths of those who attempt to cancel the gospel and the kingship of Jesus, will be silenced forever in a lake of fire.

The greatest example of the world attempting to cancel out the voice of God was their treatment of Jesus Christ. Jewish leadership listened to him just long enough to gather a charge against him, and the attacks began. They slandered him by claiming he was the illegitimate son of Mary. They claimed he was of the devil because he cast demons out of people. The Pharisees charged him with breaking the traditions of the Jewish religion. At his trial, they accused him of many things. Witnesses claimed that he said he would destroy the Temple and rebuild it in three days. They constantly demanded signs from him because they did not believe. Scribes asked Jesus questions for the purpose of impaling him on the horns of an inescapable dilemma. In the end, they crucified him using Roman authority. With all their efforts to cancel God's Son by killing him, they were powerless to stop his resurrection. Three days later, just as he had predicted, he rose from the grave to establish an eternal kingdom that will never be silence or cancelled by the hands of evil men. The victory he gained now lives in us. He has cancelled out my sin and my past forever.

As we arise each day, we are to receive the unshakable kingdom of Jesus Christ in our lives. The society we live in is a shaking mess. Wars and rumors of wars abound. The society we are living in quakes as governmental leaders come and go. Never forget that we are not a part of this world order. We have bowed to the King of glory, and we are citizens of a coming kingdom. Therefore, no man or world event can ultimately shake us off the foundation of Jesus. We are unshakable.

In retrospect, let the world go ahead and cancel us, We have canceled it a long time ago. We still live in this world, but we are no longer a part of it. We are rowing away in our life raft as the Titanic slowly descends into the depths of the icy Atlantic. One last message for the cancel culture; stop claiming you have a power you do not have and never will. When you try to cancel the voice of God, it only gets louder.

With that encouragement, I have just checked my emails and my phone messages. As far as I can tell I have received no notifications that

I have been canceled. As I sit in my easy chair looking out over God's creation, the sun has just risen in the east. Shades of light are poking into my bedroom through the window shades. I hear a mockingbird chasing a crow away from its nest. Apparently, God has not canceled the day. And so, I suppose I should get dressed and keep walking with the King. After all, this might be the day he returns.

⁊ᴍᴍᴑ

Since all these things are not to be dissolved, what sort of people are you to be in lives of holiness and godliness, waiting for and hastening the coming of the day of God, because of which the heavens will be set on fire and dissolved, and the heavenly bodies will melt as they burn!

2 PETER 3:11,12 ESV

CHAPTER 25

Friendships

Today was a sad day. I learned that an old childhood friend had died. He was a year younger and lived across the street where I grew up. He was chubby and funny and since I was older, I got to boss him around a little. We played together under his trailer and ran through hay pastures. Charlie and I rummaged through barns and climbed trees until the sun went down. Spending hours in the stream that ran behind my house, we hunted crayfish and climbed the hill that led into a dark, mysterious forest. He never did accomplish the feat of staying overnight at my house. Homesick, Charlie would jump out of bed at midnight and run home. We shared birthday parties together and planned camping trips in the forest that we never got to take. He was my first friend, and I will never forget him.

Every year, when I returned to my hometown, I would search for Charlie, but I never found him. It was as if he had fallen off the map. Then, to my surprise, we made contact and arranged to meet when I made a trip north. I had not seen my friend in over forty years, and so, I was looking forward to renewing our relationship. Unfortunately, that meeting never happened because Charlie died a month before we were to meet. I was disappointed. I didn't even know he was sick.

It's impossible to predict life's events, but one thing is certain; life is uncertain. None of us know how long we will have with those we love.

Relationships carry a sacred value that we must treasure above all else. C.S. Lewis once said, "Friendship is unnecessary, like philosophy, like art… It has no survival value; rather it is one of those things that gives value to survival."[111] "A true friend is worth all the tea in China," as my father used to say. Friendship is one of the things that makes life worth living, and it is also what brings us comfort at the point of death.

When we lay on our deathbed, we will not count our riches or assess our accomplishments. Rather, we will think back over the people that we have been blessed to call friends. Those who have helped us spiritually will enter our thoughts and warm our hearts. Those whom we have encouraged will come to mind when we face our last moments on this earth. The man who shared the gospel with me was a Navy chief. Our ship was docked in Naples, Italy, and I was visiting in a home of believers in the countryside, south of the city. He happened to be in that home, and I can still remember us sitting together on a couch as he encouraged me to receive the Lord. I resisted, but he persisted and later that day, while walking through the Italian countryside, I became a believer. He never knew of my decision to come to Christ, and so, I look forward to meeting him in Heaven. Our crowning reward will be the people who will populate the streets of gold because God used us in their lives. Nothing else will matter when we stand before our King. There is no greater way to value our friendships than sharing the love of God found in a relationship with Jesus Christ.

To help illustrate this point, the four men, who pushed their way through the crowd to get their friend to Jesus, carried more than their comrade on that stretcher. They carried within themselves the spirit of a bulldog. These men refused to give up until they got their friend to Jesus. The Lord had returned to Capernaum, and, as his custom was, he came into the house of Simon Peter. The homes back then were small, and when Jesus entered one of them, it usually broke into a Bible study. The news of his return spread through the small village, and before long, Peter's wife was scrambling for refreshments. The room was elbow to elbow with Jesus sitting before the crowd. Suddenly, straw began to fall on the Master's head, and everyone looked up. The roof panels were being removed, revealing four men with broad, toothless smiles and scraggly hair. Grabbing four ropes, the men began lowering their crippled friend down to Jesus. Most men, at this point, would see an interruption, but Jesus saw something else. He saw faith and it pleased him.

We know nothing about these four men, but of this, we are sure. They were persistent, tenacious, and determined. Nothing would stop them from getting to Jesus. No obstacle was too great. The press of the crowd did not stop them. The possibility of Jesus rejecting them carried no weight (pun intended), and the ugly looks from the Pharisees did not deter them. Not enough has been written in celebration of those four, who tore apart a ceiling, interrupted a Bible study, and changed a man's life forever. It was bulldog evangelism at its best.

Some friendships, though, surprise us. It is the people with whom we have the least in common who sometimes become our best friends. The chemistry of closeness in relationships is certainly a mystery. Friendships transcend culture, age, gender, and sometimes even extreme personality differences. As the old saying goes, opposites attract. These types of friendships are often the work of God and become the most meaningful. One such companionship occurred in the days of the Lord's ministry between a Roman centurion and his servant. In the first century, they were the original odd couple.

To understand why their friendship was so unique, we must comprehend the social structure of their day. A centurion was a battle-hardened soldier; the servant was probably a slave taken in one of his campaigns. The soldier had seen much death and suffering, and yet, he did not allow that fact to empty his heart of compassion. The servant could have become bitter over his enslavement, having been stolen away from his family by the man he served. Both men had sufficient reason to allow the circumstances of their lives to kill any possibility of their friendship together. Cast together by fate, the two had miraculously formed a bond. In fact, they became so close that when the servant became sick, the Roman centurion went to Jesus for help. Love certainly can make strange bedfellows. It is also beautiful to see how their friendship impacted others as well.

When the centurion came to Jesus, it gave him an opportunity to demonstrate his love toward a Gentile, and help his disciples overcome their nationalistic snobbery. Surprisingly, they believed that the love of God was directed to only the Jewish nation. Jesus, amazed at the faith of the centurion, remarked that he had not seen such faith, even in Israel.

The rebuke was no doubt heard loud and clear. He was also teaching his men that those who enter the Kingdom must do so by faith, not based on heritage or ancestry lines. The idea that the sons of the Kingdom (being Jews) would be cast into outer darkness, while many from the East and West would be included at the Great Feast, must have set them on their heels.

However, the greatest benefit of the friendship between this soldier and his slave was in the outcome. The centurion was brought into direct contact with Jesus. The best thing that can result from any relationship is being brought face-to-face with the Son of God. Be open to the possibility that the next person we meet might be someone who brings us closer to Jesus. Perhaps, they will help us learn something new about the Savior. God has built us for relationships. It's not just a perk of life; it's life's glorious reward. The centurion could have been cold-hearted, but he was not. The servant could have allowed his bitterness toward the Romans to fester, but he didn't.

The Bible says our lives are like sparks from a fire that fly upward and vanish.[112] We only have a few more days, and life will be over. Do you have a friend you have not seen or heard from in many years? Call them today. If possible, go see them. They may not be here tomorrow. It makes me sad that I missed an opportunity to see Charlie. He was my first friend, and I shall never forget him, but we still have time to reach out to those still living. Make what you do today count for eternity, value people.

ᏮᎻᎬᎾ

A man of many companions may come to ruin, but there is a friend who sticks closer than a brother.

PROVERBS 18:24 ESV

CHAPTER 26

Times are a Changing

In 1964, Bob Dylan released an album which included the song, *The Times They Are a-Changin*.[113] It was a short ditty which became universally popular for its lyrics that promoted societal change. Those who were opposed to the change were encouraged to get out of the way. Parents were told; "your sons and your daughters are beyond your control." The song has come full circle to mean more than it did when it was first recorded. The days we are "a-livin in" perfectly reflect Dylan's song in a way he never imagined. The times are changing for sure, and, at face value, it doesn't appear to be for good. But appearances can be deceiving. It is easy to be drawn into a state of doom over the clouds that are forming over our restless ocean of problems. The sea of humanity is churning. Let's step back for a moment and look at it with clear eyes.

Perhaps, there is something afoot in our world that will usher in a new age. We may be on the verge of a new world order that will make what we are living in now feel like an amusement park on a cool spring day. Western culture and the world at large appear to be in sharp decline, but never forget; the night is darkest just before the dawn. God has not fallen asleep at the wheel. His hand guides the rudder through the narrow passages of man's foolishness.

For those who believe in the sovereignty of God, these are the most exciting of days. When all seems lost, that's when the calvary arrives.

His return is on a fast-approaching horizon. In the interim, though, that glorious day seems a million light years away, and we can begin to feel alone and fearful. That sense of dread is nothing new. Men and women of faith have walked that same path on their way to Heaven for thousands of years.

In the book of First Kings, the story of Elijah's flight from Jezebel is recorded. The Prophet had just experienced a mighty victory on top of Mount Carmel, and was, spiritually, on top of the world. After challenging the prophets of Baal to a contest, he had soundly defeated them by calling fire down from Heaven. The sacrifice was consumed instantaneously with a fiery blast that sent the false prophets back on their heels. He then marched those evil preachers down to the Jordan River and sent their heads floating in the current. The scene looked like melons bobbing down a river in Transylvania. Then something astounding occurred. Standing amid the headless bodies on the shoreline of the river, he received a dispatch. It was a message from Jezebel, the wife of King Ahab. "Then Jezebel sent a messenger to Elijah, saying, "So may the gods do to me and more also, if I do not make your life as the life of one of them by this time tomorrow."[114] She basically put a contract out on his life.

Surprisingly, the same Prophet who stared down a herd of false preachers became terrified by an evil queen. Threatened by Jezebel, he took off on a cross-country jog and ended up in a cave in the wilderness south of Beersheba. The Lord fed him angel food cake on his journey but even that couldn't pull him out of the molligrubs. Sitting in the cave, alone and despondent, Elijah was despaired of life. He looked out over the spiritual landscape of Israel and concluded that he was the only member left in a four-man bobsled team. He reminded the Lord that he alone had been faithful to the high calling of ministry, and he was tired of his solo performance. It's easy to think we are all alone in the struggle. The enemy likes us in the cave of self-pity. Ministry is exhausting when pride slips into our hearts, and we think it's all on us. We come to believe we are God's only warrior in the fight. It is gracious of the Lord that he does not walk away from us in those moments.

In response to his terrified Prophet, God sent a mighty wind, an earthquake, and a blast of fire but in none of those things did he speak to Elijah. Finally, the Lord spoke through a still small voice. He asked

Elijah, "Why are you here in this cave?"[115] The Lord did not ask the question because he wanted information. He desired Elijah to face his fear of Jezebel and to come out of the cave. The prophet had allowed the threat of death to set him on the sideline for future exploits. Thinking he was all alone, and surrounded by the dark walls of the cave, Elijah felt outnumbered, outmaneuvered, and outgunned. He had to be reminded that he still had breath in his lungs, and therefore, the Lord was not done with him. God pulled him out of that cave by sending him on a new mission. He reminded Elijah that there were yet 7000 others who had not bowed down to Baal. He was not alone, and neither are we. Are you feeling threatened by our collapsing world? Do you feel like you are all alone? We all need encouragement to face the circumstances of the world in which we live.

First, let's face the dragon head on because fear, like a suffocating cloud, will keep you in a cave. It will cause you to think you are alone in the fight. God has plenty of warriors in the fight strategically placed and waiting for his call to battle. What appears to be hopeless is just God's opportunity to do amazing things. Remember, God and one man are always a majority.

Secondly, see the world situation with eyes of faith. Darkness *has* descended on our world. The foundations of society *are* hanging on the edge of a cliff. The daily news reads like a cheap horror novel. Unchartered waters tend to land us on shores unknown and that is why our personal perspective during difficult times is more important than the times themselves. Without a heavenly viewpoint, life can appear mighty scarry. Our faith in God is needed most when our oars are taken away and the ocean swells. The darkness is closing in, and so, I offer you a third bit of light to cheer you on your path to the eternal city. Jesus said, "I will build my church and the gates of hell will not prevail against it."[116] God is building his church through these troubled times as he has for the last 2000 years. He is using the collapsing sand to reveal that the only true foundation of life is Jesus Christ. The uncertainty that grips our world will open people's eyes to the truth. "What profit is there," asked Jesus, "if we gain the whole world and lose your own soul."[117] People, in our world today, are shaken by the changes they are experiencing. As a result, they are more open to the gospel than ever before. Now is the time to sing our loudest and longest refrain of the love of God for the souls of men. His offer of eternal life to all must be our everlasting crescendo.

God is in control. Nothing catches him off guard. He is not in Heaven ringing his hands with dismay for the future and neither should we down here on earth. He has not given us the spirit of fear as Paul reminded Timothy.[118] Jesus told his followers to, "fear not," because it is the Father's good pleasure to give them the Kingdom.[119] Our present world crisis is accomplishing his purposes. God is at work to bring about his Kingdom. The meek *shall* inherit the earth. Our responsibility is to hold forth the truth of the gospel as man's only hope. His kingdom will surely come and from appearances sooner than we may think.

⁂

For God has not given us the spirit of fear; but of power, and of love, and of a sound mind.

1TIMOTHY 1:7 KJV

CHAPTER 27

Full Steam Ahead

There are times to hit the gas, and then there are times to slam on the brake. Wise is the person who knows which pedal to choose. To accelerate in the moment, when restraint is called for, is dangerous. To hesitate, when clearly the moment cries out for immediate action, is equally disastrous. We who trust in Jesus may honestly look out over our times and ask ourselves the question, is it the brake we need or the gas pedal? Should we run for cover, circle the wagons, and wait for Jesus to pull us out of this mess or march forward into the fray giving our last breath for his cause? Is the gospel worth the fight?

It was the first time I borrowed my father's car. I was a teenager, and so, my lack of experience on the roadways was made all the worst by the overconfidence of my youth. It was a Buick Century. All was going well until I came upon a straight stretch of road and found myself behind a very slow little old lady driving a late model Ford. Seeing the dotted line before me I felt the adrenaline rush through my veins. This would be my first experience passing a car in real time. Classroom theory was in my rear window, and the pavement before me was staring me down. My father was not in the passenger seat, and so, alone to make my own decision, I hit the gas, as any self-respecting teenager would do. I pulled into the passing lane and looked over at a kind-looking elderly lady and smiled politely. I looked back in front of me, and a semi was headed toward me. I knew

I had a decision to make and only split seconds to make it. I pressed the gas harder. I suppose you could surmise from the fact that I am writing this article that I survived the event, and you would be correct. I quickly pulled the old Buick back into my lane with my heart thumping out of my chest. In that moment I decided to keep the experience to myself and to use a bit more caution the next time I was tempted to pass another car. Being careful will keep you alive on the roadways, but it has no place in the spiritual realm. We are to be risk-takers for God.

When the apostles of our Lord were threatened to keep their mouths shut concerning Jesus Christ, they immediately returned to the Temple and preached louder than before. Rather than press on the brake, they hit the gas pedal. These men realized that everything in this life is temporary, including their own lives. They understood that the eternal destinies of men and women were determinant on faith in the gospel of Jesus Christ, and that they would stop at nothing to preach Jesus louder and clearer. This is no time for stage fright. When our opportunity arises, and the curtain goes up, as it has in our culture and world today, it is time to hit the gas and open our mouths wide. The only hope for the world is Jesus Christ. There is a speed bump, though, that many times appears in the road of life, and it is fear.

Fear is debilitating. It strikes at the heart like a hot knife through butter, leaving its victim paralyzed, and worse, compliant to its commands. Fear is a deadly weapon in the hands of the powerful. Its ability to manipulate knows no equal. We bow to the unthinkable when we are afraid of possible negative outcomes. Sometimes, fear is a tool in the hands of a school-yard bully. Often it lies in the clutches of those we have elected to our land's highest posts. However, wherever it is found, fear must be recognized for what it is, a weak man's last resort. We walk as mindless robots when we are afraid, and that's the way the powerful like it. When our minds are clear, and our spirits fearless, we stand tall in difficult circumstances and against ruthless men.

Based on God's word, and the events happening around us, it is doubtful things will get better. Paul warned us that in the last days perilous times will come when men will be lovers of themselves. Narcissism has spread like a cancer throughout our world as men seek only what profits them personally. Should we run for the hills and wait for better days? No. If we choose to hide away in a cave of denial, the tentacles of terror will reach in and pull us out. If we spend these days looking outward to the events brazen across our TV screens, we will be filled with fear. It is also impossible to block out completely what's going on around us. Ostriches look silly when they poke their heads in the sand.

In the Psalms, the writer was in great distress, but rather than allowing himself to become paralyzed by fear, he lifted his heart to Heaven and called on the Lord. "They surrounded me, surrounded me on every side; in the name of the LORD, I cut them off! They surrounded me like bees; they went out like a fire among thorns; in the name of the LORD, I cut them off!"[120] Now, that sounds incredibly simple, but there is no one else who can take away our fear. The Lord answered his prayer and set him free. He realized that the Lord was on his side and if God be for us, Paul reminded us, who can stand against us?[121] The real fear has always been on the side of the enemies of God. The inhabitants of Jericho had to learn that lesson.

The Israelites had just crossed over the Jordon River on dry ground and had gathered at Gilgal. The Canaanites knew that an attack was imminent, but they were uncertain as to when and where the Jews would launch their offensive. The King of Jericho rallied his troops as panic-stricken mothers searched for their children. Old men waited for the sword to be thrust through their failing livers as soldiers sharpened their swords. Chaos filled the streets of the city. For forty years they had dreaded this day. The stories of God's deliverance of the people of Israel in the wilderness were more than folklore, they were true stories that had been told in Jericho from their childhood.

With great fear, the King of Jericho peered over the wall and saw a strange sight. About a mile away, Joshua, the leader of Israel, was holding something sharp in his hand. As he watched in astonishment, Joshua began to circumcise man after man and directed others in the same bloody operation.[122] Apparently, the Jewish rite of circumcision had not been performed in the desert for 40 years. The name Gilgal means to *roll away*. The Lord was rolling away the reproach of Egypt from his young warriors before they went into battle. As the sun set, 250,000 soldiers stumbled about Gilgal, crippled by a wound that took away their strength to fight.

A few days later the inhabitants of Jericho watched as the camp of Israel filled the plain with fire pits. They were roasting thousands of lambs in preparation for a meal of some kind. A cry, no doubt, arose in the city, "It is our chance. Fate has smiled upon us. We must go now to fight these Israelites; they are weakened by Joshua's foolishness; they are distracted by their gluttony." But the King, blinded by his evil heart, warned them that it was a trap, and the people dispersed. The prince of this world fears the gospel and the sons and daughters of the coming Kingdom more than we will ever know. It is good to be reminded of that fact.

Outside the city walls, Joshua walked alone surveying its strength and size. He looked up and saw an armed warrior. He was ordered to take off his sandals because the ground he was standing on was holy. In their conversation he was told something that changed everything. Joshua staggered back in amazement. Any doubt, concerning the upcoming campaign, was transformed into confidence by the Angel's pronouncement. Joshua's fear became courage. He was told that God had *given* Joshua the city of Jericho. No fighting was necessary. Joshua was ordered to simply walk around the city walls for seven days, and then after a shout of victory, the walls would fall.

As Joshua looked back at Jericho, he saw the same wall, standing as tall as it had only minutes before, and yet, he now viewed it with the eyes of faith. The Israelites marched around the city for seven days, blew a trumpet, and shouted. They shouted the victory that the Lord had promised, and the walls came tumbling down. Mighty Jericho was already defeated before they lifted a sword. This truth was directed toward eyes of faith. John reminds us that, "faith is the victory that overcomes the world."[123]

Our faith must never be in men. Our trust must never be directed to those in power. Our kingdom is not of this world. Only the Prince of Peace will bring peace and justice to this sinful world. Fear not, believer, this world is not our home. Stop looking out, stop looking down, and for heaven's sake, stop looking within yourself for strength to face your fears. The Lord has provided all that we need to walk throughout this world without fear. Just shout victory because Jericho has already been defeated.

Out of my distress I called on the Lord; the Lord answered me and set me free. The Lord is on my side; I will not fear. What can man do to me?

PSALM 118:5,6 ESV

CHAPTER 28

Faithful unto Death

The appeal of the gospel of God must never be directed to the need of man but to the authority and kingship of Jesus Christ. When a man hoists the banner of the King of kings over his life, he instantly becomes an enemy of the kingdoms of this world. The early disciples paid a heavy price for their faith. Should we expect anything less? The promises Jesus made to us are mostly for the life to come and that's where we should focus our attention. We deceive ourselves if we think Jesus came to give us an easy path, free from troubles. In fact, he promised that in this life we would have tribulation.[124]

There are times we find ourselves in situations we did not expect because we were not sufficiently warned or because we did not ask enough questions. Ignorance is not bliss when we are walking through a minefield. Road signs, such as the bridge is out, is not something we can afford to ignore. Regardless, being unprepared for anything is unnerving and usually leads to a bad end. As the old saying goes, "forewarned is forearmed." I was reminded of this recently from an experience I had as a young man.

At the ripe old age of seventeen I found myself in Great Lakes, Illinois in the month of February. Now, in case your geography is a little lax, that part of the country in the month of February is cold; extremely cold. Having lived in upstate New York, I thought I knew frigid temperatures, but the wind that blows off Lake Michigan in the winter is a different beast altogether. The cold, though, was not the only thing I had to face in the winter of 1977. I was in Navy boot camp. The first morning I woke up in that enchanted place, I was awakened by the sound of a metal trashcan being thrown down the middle of the barracks. My company was told to fall out of the grinder, which I later discovered was Navy jargon for a frozen parking lot. As we assembled ourselves on that icy tundra, the wind from Lake Michigan began to blow. Like ice cycle pops, we all stood at attention with the only sign of life being our breaths pumping out a cloud of white smoke. We then marched half a mile to a building with green smoke bellowing from a pipe poking out from the top of the building. A nauseating odor was coming from the pipe. The chow hall offered my new friends and I instant eggs, greasy bacon, cold toast, and lukewarm coffee. The five minutes we were allowed to eat was more than sufficient. A bellowing voice commanded us back out on the grinder to again face the angry winter wind.

As we stood at attention on the grinder, the man behind me began to choke. I became convinced that in a matter of seconds my new shipmate would deliver his half-digested breakfast on the asphalt behind me. I stood frozen in anticipation of the inevitable. When he finally hurled his green eggs and greasy bacon, I felt the warm substance hit the back of my leg and run down into my shoe. Desperately working to digest the slop I had forced down; I did everything I could not to join him in his dietary protest of vomit. Then it happened, my moment of icy discovery, when the cold hard truth came crashing in like a jarring slap in the face. I lifted my eyes to the starry night and thought, *I have gotten myself into a mess this time*. I had been promised palm trees and sandy beaches with warm breezes. The posters in the Navy recruiter's office never included the scene I was presently experiencing. I had been bamboozled.

Disappointment is unrealized expectations. We are let down, as they say, when we expected something and then experienced a different reality. We set the bar at a certain height and then life comes in below that line. When Jesus called his disciples, he warned them that they would be hated of all men, hunted down like common criminals, and in constant trouble. He made no attempt to win followers by offering them an easy ride through this world. The promises of wealth, health, and having a wonderful, carefree life, were absent from Jesus' teachings. In fact, he offered them nothing from this world but a punch in the nose.

The fife and drum, used in the Revolutionary War by both sides, were more than a musical reprieve from the horrors of the battlefield. The drum especially was used as a means of giving direction on the battlefield. David Hackett Fischer, in his book, *Washington's Crossing*, records the discipline needed in the British army in reference to the cadence of the drum while in battle. "Recruits also learn to respond willingly to the beat of the drum… In 1768, Thomas Sime's, *The Military Medley*, listed many drum signals that each British soldier had to learn… Many signals were for maneuvers on the battlefield. One stroke with a flam (made by striking the drumhead with both drumsticks almost but not quite simultaneously) meant turn or face right. Two strokes and a flam meant turn left. Three strokes were the signal for turning right about four meant left about. Altogether British regiments used 170 drum signals, and soldiers were drilled to move instantly on hearing them."[125] As the bullets and cannonballs flew by the soldiers, it was easy for men to become temporally insane. The fife and drum were used to help men keep their *presence of mind* amid the battle. With the warnings and promises Jesus made to us, he has done the same.

As Jesus spent time with his disciples, he told them that in this world they would have tribulation, but to be of good cheer, because he had overcome the world. When Paul wrote Timothy, he warned him that in the last days perilous times would come. He cautioned that men would be lovers of themselves, lovers of money, proud, and the list went on and on.[126] Jesus told the church at Smyrna, "Do not fear what you are about to suffer. Behold, the devil is about to throw some of you into prison, that you may be tested, and for ten days you will have tribulation. Be faithful unto death, and I will give you the crown of life."[127] Jesus warned us of the battle ahead, and in doing so, he helps us keep our, "presence of mind."

As we share Christ in this world, we do men no justice by sharing a diluted gospel linked to promises our Lord never made. The current of this world flows in one direction, and when someone chooses to walk in opposition to it, resistance is the natural reaction. The end times will be brutal, but he has promised to never leave us or forsake us. He told the church of Smyrna to be faithful unto death, and he would give them the crown of life. Six out of the seven churches in the book of Revelation were given a specific promise all their own. Ephesus was promised that they would eat of the Tree of Life in God's paradise, while Smyrna was assured that they would not be hurt by the second death. Pergamum would be given a new name, and Thyatira would receive the Morning Star. The Philadelphians were assured they would be made a pillar in the temple of their God, and Sardis was told they would wear white garments. Only the church at Laodicea was left without a promise.

Despite our circumstances, Jesus demands complete loyalty, and he expects his followers to renounce all worldly possession and allegiances. Rather than offer the smooth life of convenience, Jesus wisely prepares his followers for the inevitable conflict ahead. "Do you think that I have come to bring peace," he asked his disciples. "I have come to bring a sword to divide men along the line of spiritual conflict."[128] As he walked along the shoreline of the Sea of Galilee, he told Peter to drop his nets and come follow him. When the rich, young ruler walked away disappointed, the Master made no attempt to go after him. The high standard of complete devotion to God and renunciation of all wealth was seen by that man as too high a price to pay, and Jesus never lowered that edict. Our highest devotion must be to Christ, and if that means the offering of our life in death, then so be it because he is worthy.

Woe to you, when all people speak well of you, for so their fathers did to the false prophets.

LUKE 6:26 ESV

CHAPTER 29

The Lion and the Lamb

Writers and readers alike call it the plot twist. It is the moment in the story that you never saw coming. Connecting the dots of the tale, you were sure that it would flow in a particular direction, and then out of nowhere everything changes. Suddenly, the characters are sent in new directions. Plot twists make the story both interesting and exciting. When a story becomes predictable, we put the book down and turn off the lights. Dorothy's life, on a Kansas plain is mundane until a tornado plows through the farm and lifts her tiny house into the sky. When the evil spell of a witch turns a prince into a beast, the story begins. Until a girl named Alice follows a white bunny down a rabbit hole, the tale is just about a child falling asleep in a meadow. When the plot twist comes, the story itself takes on a new hue as old characters are seen in a new light. The hero becomes the villain, and the village beggar was really a doctor hiding from an unfortunate past. Luke Skywalker finds out that Darth Vader was his father, and Professor Severus Snape ends up protecting Harry Potter. The skinny kid saves the day through his superior intellect, and the beautiful maiden is really a witch in disguise. A story, without a plot twist, is hardly worth our time.

From the dawn of time, civilization has been searching for a hero, a plot twist character, who will steer our world in a better direction. The list goes back as far as Eve's first son, Abel. His mother proudly announced,

"I have gotten a man from the Lord."[129] Literally, the Hebrew reads *the* man. Eve believed she had given birth to the promised Messiah. What a disappointment that was as Cain killed his own brother. The parade of possible redeemers continued with Nimrod and included characters such as Nebuchadnezzar, Alexander the Great, Julius Caesar, and in our day, Joseph Stalin, and Adolf Hitler. Every new king who ascends the throne, as well as every politician who gets elected, is crowned to bring us all a better life with a new society. These self-acclaimed saviors are at least consistent; they all either fall flat or become corrupt with the power they are given. In the worst extremity, they become tyrants and dictators who murder millions of innocent people. In the least, they all turn out to be as flavorless as tapioca and as useless as a vegetarian chef in a steak house.

Clearly, the world we live in is on the verge of a major plot twist. Humanity is anxiously awaiting some shocking moment that will usher in a new age. The apostle John caught a glimpse of that moment when he was an old man on the island of Patmos. He stood before the God of Heaven and saw a scroll that was sealed with seven seals. An angel suddenly cried out, "Who is worthy to open the scroll and break its seals?"[130] He waited, but no one answered. Not a peep in Heaven, or on earth, or under the earth. John wept. Mankind had been searching for a hero, and now their last hope was gone. John felt the agony that humanity and all creation had been experiencing for thousands of years, and it was overwhelming.

An Elder stepped forward and told John to dry his tears. "Weep no more; behold, the Lion of the tribe of Judah, the Root of David, has conquered, so that he can open the scroll and its seven seals."[131] The pressure in his chest released as his shoulder felt the weight of a thousand burdens lift. John, in a flash of insight, understood the significance of what he was witnessing. The scroll he saw contained the blueprints of a new world order with one supreme ruler. This scroll, and its seven seals, would unleash God's judgement on sin and usher in a new society wherein righteousness reigns.

However, what he saw next shocked him. The scene was astounding. John expected to see some great conquering army, led by a powerful commander, but he witnessed a jaw-dropping plot twist. Instead of a Lion he saw a Lamb! A deeper paradox cannot be imagined as John looked at the One who had died, in full command of God's plan for mankind and the future of the new created order. As the Lamb took the scroll from the One who sat on the throne, a celebration of worship began that shook the courts of Heaven and moved it like a mighty flood across all of creation.[132] Jesus, who had been crucified on a cross, would now rule and reign, and as a result, all men would be directed toward the only One who is worthy of worship and honor.

It is vital we keep this plot twist firmly in our minds as we approach the coming days. Daily bombarded by the images of a world gone mad, it is easy to slip into depression and despondency. It is easy to become disillusioned and discouraged in these last days when everything seems bleak. The Bible calls the days we are living in, "perilous times."[133] Likewise, the temptation to look to this world for hope is strong. If we allow our minds to be filled with worldly concerns, then we will dig a hole and bury ourselves in our sorrows. If we believe Jesus came to build his kingdom on the crumbling foundations of this world, then we will take up the banner of saving our nation instead of staying busy preaching the gospel. There is the temptation to trust political processes and personalities to remedy societal declines. By doing this, we waste our time building sandcastles all the while ignoring the incoming tide of God's kingdom. It is possible to adopt the false hope that God favors a particular nation or people. The first disciples had fallen into that trap.

Moments before Jesus ascended back to Heaven his followers asked one last time concerning the restoration of the kingdom to Israel. The hope that Israel would become a great world power was a dream that none of them were willing to give up. They really believed that the purpose of Jesus was to rescue their national identity and propel them into places of power over an earthly kingdom. They were wrong. The vision Jesus wanted them to embrace was not limited to a nation but for the entire world. The advancement of any worldly kingdom was never his mission. He came to redeem humanity. He left the glories of Heaven to make men right for the streets of the New Jerusalem. He came to build his church by redeeming men and women from all nations.

Consequently, when our minds are set on Christ, and our eyes are focused on the heavens for his return, no storyline from the nightly news will dishearten us. The world we are witnessing is as flimsy as a house made of cards and as fragile as a papier-mâché castle. As this world crumbles around us, the eternal kingdom of God draws closer. Like Nebuchadnezzar's statue in the book of Daniel, the Rock of Heaven will fall, crushing all world governments. Jesus will set up his Millennial kingdom in Jerusalem and rule the world with a rod of iron for a thousand years. The creation will be set free from the curse of Adam's sin and bloom as we have never seen it. The lion will lay down with the lamb, and a child will play with a once poisonous snake. The promise Jesus made that we shall inherent the earth will come to pass as we reign with Christ on this earth.

Our glorious future is secure because of the great plot twist of the crucifixion. Keep your mind on Christ, and nothing but joyful anticipation will fill your heart. He's coming in the clouds. Every eye will see him, and those who have chosen to follow him will reap the reward of eternal life. In that day, we will shine as the stars in the heavens, reflecting the glory of our King.

Then I looked, and behold, on Mount Zion stood the Lamb...

REVELATION 14:1 ESV

CHAPTER 30

Wonder

Aiden Wilson Tozer was a minister of the gospel in Alliance Churches throughout the Northeast. His books have blessed millions because he wrote with honesty and toughness regarding spiritual matters. Tozer pulled no punches. In his book, *The Knowledge of the Holy*, he writes this concerning worship, "What enters our minds when we think about God is the most important thing about us. The history of mankind will probably show that no people have ever risen above its religion, and man's spiritual history will positively demonstrate that no religion has ever been greater than its idea of God. Worship is pure or base as the worshiper entertains high or low thoughts of God."[134] According to Tozer, we were created to experience a sense of awe and wonder as we contemplate the majesty of the incomprehensible God. Mankind was created to become gloriously obsessed with his Maker.

In contrast, Narcissus was a hunter in Greek Mythology who was obsessed only with himself. He was a handsome young man who attracted the attention of many maidens. However, Narcissus treated all his suitors with distain and contempt. While hunting in the woods, a nymph named Echo spotted him and fell deeply in love. Hiding in the shadows, she finally revealed her true feelings and attempted to hug Narcissus. Casting her aside, she was told not to bother him. Deeply hurt, she ran into the thicket where she hid for the rest of her days. Only the trace of her voice could be heard from what remained of the young woman. Nemesis, the Greek god of revenge was angered and cursed Narcissus in the following manner. While looking into a pond, the hunter fell in love with his reflection, not aware he was looking at his own image. By the time he realized what was happening, it was too late. He was doomed for the rest of his life to be consumed with himself at the expense of all others. Behold, the Achilles' heel of mankind. We are all in love with ourselves. Some hide it better than others, but the fact remains.

Narcissism, to one degree or another, affects us all. From the moment we were born, our entire life's aim was to be taken care of by someone other than ourselves. All the world was our oyster, and everyone we encountered held a shucking blade. The very first job of every parent is to drive this selfishness far from the child. My father informed me early in life that my purpose on earth was to serve him, and I think that helped me in some strange way. It is the desire of God to redirect our self-absorbed spirit toward the One who is worthy of attention.

Our two-year old granddaughter, Adeline, is obsessed with the moon. Day or night, when she spots that mysterious ball in the sky, she stops, points, and loudly exclaims, "the moon, the moon." So, you can only imagine her delight last week when she entered Epcot for the first time. There it was, sitting on the ground before her, the moon. Adeline lifted her hands and squealed. Her mother, recognizing the situation, began to explain that it was not, in fact, the moon. But then she stopped. Rather than take away the joy of her daughter's great discovery, she leaned down and whispered in her ear, "Yes, honey, that's the moon." The celebration that followed was a thing to behold as her family watched Adeline dance and shout with great delight. Her celebration reminded me of a truth that we need to rediscover.

Pull back the curtain and peer into the heavenly scenes, given to us by Scripture, and you will be astounded by their grandeur. The songs we hear in those celestial courts are simple with a singular focus on the worthiness and greatness of God. They ring with the power of pure adoration. When the apostle John saw a vision of the son of God in his glory, he fell as a dead man.[135] Later, in the Revelation he listened as the four living creatures cry out, "Holy, holy, holy, is the Lord God Almighty, who was and is and is to come."[136] In response to their proclamation of God's glory, the twenty-four elders fall before the throne and cast their crowns at his feet. As they worship, they say, "Worthy are you, our Lord and God, to receive glory and honor and power, for you created all things, and by your will they existed and were created."[137]

The stories of these men, who received the blessing of seeing God's glory, amazes us. However, notice all their attention is placed on God, not on themselves. Our true need is to worship the One who overwhelms us. The prophet Daniel fell as a dead man in the presence of the Angel of the Lord.[138] Peter was so befuddled on the Mount of Transfiguration that he offered to build booths.[139] When the prophet Isaiah witnessed the glory of God, filling the temple, he was so overwhelmed that he pleaded for the vision to depart saying, "I am a man of unclean lips."[140] The list could go on and on, but in all these visions, the glory of man fades, and the One who deserves true worship bursts on the scene in unapproachable light. The worshiper is suddenly lost in wonder. Narcissism evaporates in the presence of the One who deserves our full attention.

God has placed within mankind the desire and ability to worship. Until we come face to face with Jesus Christ, we worship all the wrong things and for all the wrong reasons. No man is ready to live until he is overtaken by Someone greater than himself. We must be conquered by the unspeakable glory of the Lord before we enter a life of wonder. When the Holy Spirit reveals Jesus to a man or woman, they are never the same again.

Adeline danced with joy when she saw the object of her desire close enough to touch. Jesus said, "Behold the Kingdom of God is among you."[141] Are you dancing today concerning his Kingdom? Our granddaughter could have cared less who was watching because she was lost in wonder. This is how we finish our race with joy. In the presence of the glorious God, the glory of man wilts like a dandelion pulled up from its roots. No man can be impressed with himself once he sees Jesus Christ.

⊙〰〰〰〰9

Looking unto Jesus the author and finisher of our faith, who for the joy that was set before him endured the cross, despising the shame, and is set down at the right hand of the throne of God.

HEBREWS 12:2 KJV

CHAPTER 31

Armadillo Wars

S ome people question why God created mosquitoes; I often wonder why he made armadillos. Ugly, armored, warriors of the night, they can transform a backyard into a war zone. Grunting as they forage for grubs and mole crickets, these heartless possums in a half shell, easily create a mini minefield for an unsuspecting homeowner. Oh, and did I mention, they also carry human leprosy. If all this sounds a bit personal, it's because, well, it is. I have been at war with these miniature Sherman tanks of terror, and my patience is growing thin. Traps, repellants, motion lights and even sirens don't slow them down, they just keep coming.

Armadillos are destructive creatures, but there is something more devastating than these evil rodents that rule the darkness. There is a source of despair more relentless than these pesty nighttime commandos. It is living with regret and shame. Sunny days are turned into unrelenting rainstorms when these two unwelcomed intruders live in the basement of our lives. The unseen power of shame and regret holds us hostage, refusing any promise of freedom from their clutches. Shame points to our weakest moments and attempts to define us. Regret amplifies our past failures to hinder us from being used by God in the future. The physical toll these twin monsters take is a greater threat than those posed by an army of armadillos. Furthermore, we rarely slow down long enough to think about the toll they take on our lives. Is there any hope for those caught in the web of the self-destructive outflow of shame and regret?

When Peter stood to preach on the day of Pentecost, he was fresh off a total melt-down of faith. After having denied the Lord three times, he could have packed his bags and headed north to Galilee. No one would have blamed Peter if he had chosen to go back to his fishing nets. He chose, instead, to remain with the other disciples and wait in Jerusalem. For fifty days Peter owned his denial of Jesus without making the first excuse. He then stepped out onto a rooftop in Jerusalem, and boldly proclaimed the good news of salvation before thousands of his fellow Jews. All the other disciples knew about his failure, and yet, they stood with him as he became their leader in proclaiming grace and forgiveness. Peter stood on that great day and fished for men. He could have chosen to allow guilt to silence him, but instead, Peter preached like a man who had nothing to lose but God's glory. After his denial, Peter stood and spoke with confidence. He possessed the boldness of a lion. He cast a huge net as thousands repented and were brought into the kingdom of God. Peter decided to reject self-pity and shame in exchange for a second chance at life.

There were two driving forces that propelled Peter back into the fight. First, he believed he had been completely forgiven and fully restored by Jesus. Paul mentioned a private meeting between Peter and the Lord after his resurrection.[142] We are not told what was said, but I would have loved to be privy to that conversation. Peter had been given the gift of seeing what was in his heart, and it wasn't pretty. Perhaps, he felt happier alone on the Sea of Galilee catching fish. Perchance, he wished he had never left his nets. He was strong enough for the rigors of his boats and nets, but Jesus was sending him to greater waters. Regardless of how he felt, Peter's failure had a purpose. His lowest moment was God's greatest opportunity. If he was going to be the kind of fisherman Jesus needed, he had to stop trusting himself and begin looking to Christ for everything. His confidence had to be taken off his shoulders and placed on the One who was more than sufficient to carry the burden.

In his offer of mercy Jesus never blinked and Peter never hesitated to forgive himself. The big fisherman from Galilee had come to understand how small he was in the task that was about to be placed upon him. Self-confidence was gone, and in its place, total trust in his Lord. Men that are dealing with shame and regret never venture onto the battlefield. Peter had experienced grace, and so, it was grace that he preached.

Secondly, the day of Pentecost had arrived and with it the coming of the Holy Spirit. The change it wrought in those men was inexplicable. Eleven timid disciples suddenly found the courage to face a large Jewish crowd in the same city where their Master had recently been crucified. It would have made more sense to establish the church in Galilee where all the disciples were more comfortable, but God has always done his best work in the belly of the beast. In the face of the Sanhedrin, and the Roman authorities, thousands were saved, as the church was born. In the same city where the darkness of his crucifixion had occurred, the light of the gospel broke out, and it was Peter who led the charge.

Jesus promised that after he had gone back to his Father, greater works would be done by those who believed. The return of Jesus to Heaven meant that God had accepted his work on the cross. The life and work of Jesus could now be given to the men and women who had chosen to follow him. The Holy Spirit came down, and that group in the upper room came alive. What Jesus had done *for* them could now be manifest *in* them. Peter was filled with the Holy Spirit when he preached, "This same Jesus, whom you crucified, is both Lord and God."[143] The forgiveness, restoration, and the unction of the Holy Spirit empowered Peter to see boldly into the future and step out in faith. Do you clearly see the victory that God has accomplished on your behalf? "For God gave us a spirit not of fear but of power and love and self-control."[144]

On the day that the sun stood still, Joshua and the armies of Israel pursued five kings of the Canaanites. These kings fled and hid themselves in a cave at Makkedah. When it was told to Joshua, he commanded his men to place large stones over the mouth of the cave. After defeating the enemy armies, he took his commanders to the cave and brought the five kings out. Forcing them to lay down on the ground, he told his warrior chiefs to place their feet on their necks. "And Joshua said to them, 'Do not be afraid or dismayed; be strong and courageous. For thus the Lord will do to all your enemies against whom you fight."[145] Joshua then killed all five kings and had them hung in a tree for all to witness the victory of God. Fear is overcome by focusing on the power of God, not our meager resources. Faith places our spiritual foot on the necks of shame and regret.

Evan Hopkins, author of *The Law of Liberty in the Spiritual Life,* wrote this concerning God's superiority over our enemy. "Christ does not bring the believer into the valley while the enemy is occupying the heights. The conflict does not consist in obtaining the victory with His aid and dislodging the enemy from his vantage ground. The character of the conflict is completely different. To see what Christ has accomplished by *His* victory is to see that the enemy has already been overcome and dislodged from his strong hold, and that our conflict consists in fighting not *for* this position of victory but *from* it."[146] We march forward toward a defeated enemy. We shout the victory, and the walls fall down.

There is only one remedy for an armadillo, and it is a twelve-gauge shotgun. They will destroy any trap you set for them and chuckle at the repellent you put in the yard. It is the same for shame and guilt. Extreme measures are needed to move confidently forward. We cannot move ourselves out of the mud. Only God can rescue us from shame and regret. By his grace, he gives us a constant flow of victory. Until we understand how forgiven we are and how much he desires to use us, regardless of our past, these two terrors of destruction will continue to root up our lives and make it impossible to be used of God. Belief in the grace of God will set us free from the armadillos of our past or present failures. The Lord Jesus has forgiven all our sins and we glorify him most by fully forgiving ourselves. "If God is for us who can be against us."[147]

ഝൡൟ

For God gave us a spirit not of fear but of power and love and self-control.

2 TIMOTHY 1:7 ESV

CHAPTER 32

Short People

In 1977, Randy Newman recorded a song titled, *Short People*. It was a playful ditty intended to rebuke people who were short tempered, short of vision, and small of heart. Whatever his original intent, Newman utterly failed in this regard. Instead, he appears to poke fun at those who are vertically challenged. He sings about tiny little noses and tiny little eyes. He croons of those who wear platform shoes on their nasty little feet. The chorus rings out with the conclusion that short people, "got no reason to live." The song was quite funny, at least to tall people. But I am here to tell you, having married a short person, that they should never be underestimated. Jesus certainly didn't when he spotted a short Jewish man sitting in a sycamore tree.

As most of us are familiar, his name was Zacchaeus, and he lived in a city called Jericho. Lined with palm trees and fine buildings, it was a beautiful town located in the Jordan valley. One late summer day Jesus was passing through on his way to Jerusalem. Being a tax collector, Zacchaeus decided to close shop early and wade into a crowd that was rapidly forming on the main throughfare. Normally, he avoided crowded places due to the real possibility of being elbowed in the forehead or being tripped over by the crowd. You see, Zacchaeus was short. As the children's song goes, *Zacchaeus was a wee little man, and a wee little man was he. He climbed up in a sycamore tree for the Lord he wanted to see.*

Zacchaeus worked his way through the crowd that day to get a look at this miracle working carpenter from Nazareth. Like the rest of the city, he had heard all the stories and wanted to see firsthand what all the buzz was about. Hopping up and down he looked for a group of children to join to get a good vantage point. Unable to find an opening in the crowd he spotted a sycamore tree in the distance. He ran ahead and climbed onto a comfortable branch. Zacchaeus watched as Jesus passed by, and when he did, the Master looked up and smiled. His determination had paid off. His reward was to receive Jesus as a house guest that very day.[148] Ignoring the disgusted faces in the crowd, he quickly climbed down and ran to prepare a meal. You see, Zacchaeus had to overcome something more than his height restriction. He was a tax collector, and thus, hated by the people of Jericho. Of all houses to host a meal for this young rabbi from Nazareth, this would have been the last choice of Jesus' disciples.

As you might imagine, a man like Zacchaeus could throw only one kind of party, and it was exactly the sort of gathering that Jesus loved to attend. The only friends he had were outcasts like himself, and since Zacchaeus had no interest in impressing Jesus, that's who was invited. Long after the crowds in Jericho went home, Zacchaeus and his rowdy bunch of hooligans were reveling in the company of Jesus. They shared the stories of their lives and listened to the Master teach them about God's love. They laughed, sang, and danced the night away with a religious man who was anything but stiff and aloof. The Pharisees rarely gave them the time of day. Jesus had all the time in the world to listen to their hopes and dreams. He taught them about the love of his Heavenly Father.

With an over-flowing heart of gratitude, Zacchaeus interrupted the feast to make a special announcement. With the raising of his glass, he promised to repay anyone he had wronged and to give away half his wealth to the poor.[149] Cheers rang out through the windows of his home and filled the quiet streets of Jericho. The acceptance that the dinner guests experienced changed their lives. The short tax collector had never stood taller than he did that night. He was finally free from the love of money and liberated from what any man might think of him. No doubt, others still looked down on him and hated him for his chosen occupation, but none of that mattered to him now. He had experienced the love of God, and the glory of that love made everything else irrelevant. Zacchaeus finally viewed himself in the full light of Jesus Christ and he felt loved and valued.

There is no mention of the disciples in this story of Zacchaeus. Perhaps, when the party was going on, they sat quietly in the shadows. This wasn't the first time that Jesus had spent time with questionable characters, and maybe their patience was running thin. These types of people did nothing to advance their cause. If they were ever to be free from Rome, then the Messiah would need to target his work toward the rich and famous. Men like Zacchaeus only served to discredit the reputation of Jesus. Forgiving a woman caught in adultery projected an image of questionable standards on the part of Jesus. At least the time he spent with the Samaritan woman at the well could be kept quiet, they all agreed. I can see Peter whispering in James's ear as they entered Zacchaeus's house, "Here we go again."

In his earthly ministry Jesus gravitated toward outcasts and sinners because they were open to his grace and mercy. We are who God declares us to be in his estimation, not our own. We are created by a loving God for the purpose of glorifying him and enjoying his friendship. This love is bestowed by him, apart from anything we will ever say or do. He loves us because he has chosen to do so. Regardless of our social status, physical appearance, people group, or talent level, we are all created in the image of God and thus worthy of his love. Mankind will, at times, devalue us, but thank God our Father in Heaven see us all as priceless gems.

Wherever Jesus went, he caused a ruckus. In this case, rather than visiting a dignitary from the city, Jesus chose to be entertained by a house full of societal outcasts. Zacchaeus' life was not changed by following the rules of men nor the dictates of the Jewish religion. He was altered deeply when he encountered the Son of God. The kindness and love of Jesus caused Zacchaeus to cast away his greedy ways and gladly surrender. The society of Samaria, in their pious bigotry, had treated Zacchaeus as a traitor and an outcast. They evaluated him on his externals and found him unworthy of their love and acceptance. In contrast, Jesus reached out his arms and embraced him. After that day, the wee little man of Jericho had plenty of reason to live. From the branches of that sycamore tree, Zacchaeus scampered down, and became the richest man in town.

⌒◌◌◌◌◌

And behold, there was a man named Zacchaeus.

LUKE 19:2 ESV

CHAPTER 33

Death's Door

According to Ben Franklin, death is as sure as taxes. Death is a part of life, and something our culture used to more comfortable talking about. Not too many years ago funerals were held in the home of the deceased, with the casket sitting in the front living room for days. Food was enjoyed and memories were shared as the dearly departed lay cold as a cucumber in the parlor. Back then, medical advances didn't prolong the process of death. People died of old age, and no one was allowed to suffer needlessly. People were given the gift of a dignified death. Loved ones grieved and then moved on with their lives, in most cases, but not all.

There were and still are people who allow the death of a loved one to stop them cold in their tracks. For whatever reason, the passing of their beloved has left them frozen in time. Rooms, filled with memories are not disturbed, cars, driven by the deceased, are not sold, and clothes, once worn by one who no longer needs them, are neatly tucked away, or hung in a closet to collect dust. New relationships, as well as new ventures, are difficult if not impossible to forge. Death always takes the wind out of our sails, but for some, the breeze never blows again, and the sails are never hoisted. How does this happen? Is there a common thread running through this familiar, and yet, sad scenario? If moving on after a person dies is healthy and good, why do some have such a hard time?

Joshua was Moses' right-hand man. He is described in the Bible as a devoted pupil, a righteous man, and a brilliant military leader. He was also his successor who eventually led the people of God into the land of promise. Joshua, though, had an Achilles' heel regarding Moses. The writer of the book of Exodus informs us that, "when Moses turned again into the camp, his assistant Joshua the son of Nun, a young man, would not depart from the tent."[150] They appeared to be joined at the hip in what psychologists' call, "unhealthy fusion." This young man was so devoted to the leader of Israel that he allowed Moses to change his name. Joshua was so reliant on Moses that he became lethargic after his death. He had developed a weakness within that nearly crippled him from leading the nation. Unable to move on, the Lord was forced to confront Joshua. God finally declared in flat tones marked with concision, "Moses my servant is dead. Now therefore arise, go over this Jordan, you and all this people, into the land that I am giving to them, to the people of Israel."[151] Joshua needed to hear the finality of that announcement. Eulogies are read at funerals for the purpose of giving family and loved one's closure. We can learn much from Joshua's life regarding the death of a loved one.

First, until the fact of death is acknowledged, there is no moving forward in life. I can remember the words of my mother as if it were yesterday. I was a young boy who had just realized that someday I would die. I needed to be comforted, and her words hit the mark. My mother simply told me, "If you worry about death, you will not enjoy living." It was all I needed to relieve my fears. She gave me no long explanations concerning the afterlife or big words I didn't understand. Her wisdom sent me off to play with my friends and to enjoy the day. For the moment, at least, she had relieved my fears. Memory lane makes for a pleasant stroll from time to time, but it is a horrible place to live because we live there alone. By sitting in the dark room of yesterday, we close ourselves off from those who need us most.

Second, our identity must never be wrapped up in another human being no matter how precious they may be to us. Years later I stood at my mother's bedside as she was dying. Tears began to fill my eyes. Unable to speak, my mother rebuked me with stern eyes. She was saying, do not mourn for me, I am going to a better place. Now, go live your life. I have attempted to live up to her request ever since.

Thirdly, nothing of God dies when a man of God dies. The Lord's work continues through other men. As a pastor, I have seen some strange things at funerals. I have watched families, who were believers, grieve as if Heaven were not a real place. I have witnessed those, who ought to know better, act as if death were the final stop on a train ride that ran off the tracks. They blamed doctors and hospitals for their loved one's death. By dismissing the sovereignty of God, they conveniently forget that it is appointed unto man once to die. I understand the heartache of saying goodbye to those we love, especially when the young are taken from us. However, in the end, death should be a victory shout for those who know Christ.

The first century Christians viewed death from that vantage point. To them death was an entrance into the glorious presence of Christ. They released their last breath with the anticipation of breathing in the fresh air of Heaven. They faced death like an athlete, who, after crossing the finish line, would claim the victor's crown. The apostle Paul asked, "O death, where is your sting? O grave where is your victory?"[152] As far as Paul was concerned, the evil duo of death and the grave had lost their hold on those who walk with the conquering King. James was thrust through with the sword of King Herod. Stephen was stoned to death while looking into the heavens with glory on his face. Paul declared at the end of his life that he was ready to be offered, and soon after, his head rolled off a block onto a side street in Rome. Peter was crucified upside down at his own request. None of these men were afraid of death.

As the hymnwriter, Albert E. Brumley penned, *This world is not my home, I'm just a passin through,* says the old song. And since my treasures are laid up, *somewhere beyond the blue,* I hold everything in this life loosely. I look forward to the day when I will see the face of the One who died for me. I will gladly exchange the life that I have down here for a higher stage. Until then, my heart will go on singing. God has numbered my days, and I do not fear the final tally.

When the perishable puts on the imperishable,
and the mortal puts on immortality, then
shall come to pass the saying that is written:
Death is swallowed up in victory. O death, where
is your sting? O grave, where is your victory?

I CORINTHIANS 15:54,55 ESV

CHAPTER 34

Origins

almon are amazing creatures. Every autumn they return to the place of their birth, making a journey that is both difficult and dangerous. Having spent their adult lives in saltwater, they battle the strong currents of freshwater rivers to spawn. Avoiding grizzly bears, eagles, and anglers, they return to the very stream of their birth. The salmon instinctively know their place of origin, and so does man. We intuitively know we were created by God.

"In the beginning God created..."[153] This simple, and yet, profound opening verse to the greatest book ever written, teaches us a very important truth about our Creator. God is the origin of all things. Nothing comes into existence before he wills it to be so. Our next breath, as well as our next heartbeat, occurs because he chooses it to happen. God is the foundation and source of life. He initiates, we participate. He is the *First Cause,* as the ancient Greek philosophers taught. God is the *Unmoved Mover.*

Furthermore, the author of Genesis makes no attempt to convince the reader of the reality of God's existence. He simply declares, "In the beginning God..."[154] He assumes the reader already believes God exists, otherwise, there would be no reason to read the next verse. The aim of the Word of God is not to prove the existence of God. The Bible is a book of heavenly facts that require faith to receive. We must believe to understand, not vice versa. "And without faith it is impossible to please

Him, for whoever would draw nigh to God must believe that he exists and that he rewards those who seek Him."[155] The belief that God exists is reliant on faith, not tangible evidence. The path forward, spiritually, is clearly marked for those who chose to have faith in a God they cannot see. Biblical faith rests on the moral choice of the individual.

Although the Bible gives no evidence of God's existence, the world we live in reverberates with his powerful presence. Sir Isaac Newton wrote, "All variety of created objects represent order, and life in the universe could happen only be the willful reasoning of its original Creator, whom I call the 'Lord God.'"[156] The Palmist stated, "The heavens declare the glory of God, and the sky above proclaims his handiwork."[157] The testimony of creation paints an undeniable picture of a Creator God. If you came across a turtle sitting on a fence post, you would naturally wonder who placed it there. It is not a far stretch, as we witness the sheer force and magnificence of the world around us, to ask the same question.

Regardless of man's reaction to the overwhelming body of evidence, God is still the origin, the starting place for everything. Man's refusal to believe does not affect God in the least. The Bible describes him as the Alpha, which means nothing happens without him starting the process. Each day begins with the sun being called out of its slumber, and every sunset is his decision that the day is done. He is the force which causes the rooster to crow as Peter discovered. He commands the fish of the sea much to the chagrin of Jonah. In the same way, the salvation of any individual begins with the knock of God on that person's heart.

Now if we believe he is the Alpha, it naturally progresses that he is also the Omega, the One who ultimately fulfills and finishes all things. As God began the first chapter of mankind's story, he will finish the last chapter and bring the tale to resolution. Granted, his story has gotten a bit messy with the entrance of sin, but never doubt that in the end, sin will be fully eradicated. Sin will not ultimately frustrate the plan of God for man. But what is his plan?

The new creation that is coming will be established in righteousness. This storyline, which began with the promised Messiah in the Garden of Eden, was accomplish by the death and resurrection of Jesus Christ. His mission will be culminated when he appears in the clouds upon his return. Every eye will see him, and the question of his existence will be put to rest for all eternity. Those who reject his right to rule in this world, and in their lives, will have an abrupt awakening. Even those in power cannot escape his hand as one Old Testament king discovered.

In the book of Daniel, the story is told of Belshazzar, the king of Babylon and his decision to throw a party to end all parties.[158] All the high princes and people of authority were invited. An unlimited buffet was offered; the wine flowed freely, and subsequently; the feast quickly turned into a drunken orgy. At this point, the king called for the sacred vessels from the house of God in Jerusalem to be brought into the banqueting room. A stilled hush settled over the crowd. Everyone watched as Belshazzar drank from the sacred cup and defied the God of Israel. Suddenly, a hand appeared from nowhere and wrote a mysterious message into the plaster wall of the king's palace room. As the blood drained from Belshazzar's face, he dropped the vessel onto the floor and called for all the wisemen of Babylon to decipher the message. However, the writing remained a conundrum until the prophet Daniel was summoned. The Prophet, who had once been thrown to the lions, once again entered the lion's den without a hint of fear.

Daniel walked into the ballroom to read the writing and interpret its meaning. He read, "MENE, MENE, TEKEL, PARSIN; MEME: God has numbered the days of your kingdom and brought it to an end. TEKEL: You have been weighed in the balances and found wanting. PARSIN: Your kingdom is divided and given to the Medes and Persians."[159] The prophet Daniel pronounced the judgment of God over this wicked king. At that very moment, Darius and the army of the Medes and Persians were marching under the great Babylonian wall. The king thought he was safe within his mighty fortress, but when God decrees judgment, there is nowhere to hide. Belshazzar died that night with little time to prepare.

The handwriting concerning the judgment of God on this world is clearly on the wall. His return will be swift and his judgment sure. The Alpha of creation will soon be the Omega of his great return to this earth to put away sin and establish a kingdom of righteousness. Mankind's story on this present earth will finally have the ending God desires. A man is not ready to live until he is prepared to die. Until the great question of our origin has been answered, our destiny hangs in the balance. The answer to that question will not be found by looking within, we must lift our eyes to the Heavens. Only the Bible will lead us back to our Creator.

Salmon are anadromous, which is a Greek word meaning to, *run upward*. Mankind knows he has been created by God and must look *upward* to discover his origin. To live as if God did not exist is to commit eternal suicide. To refuse to believe in God's existence reveals a willful ignorance on the part of man. To think that the miracle of life crawled out of a primordial swamp is dishonesty at its deepest level. Those who question God's existence are being morally dishonest with themselves. They are denying what is staring them in the face, all the while continuing down a path of moral decay. If we refuse to swim upstream, we will remain in the saltwater of sin and corruption. To live, as if God did not exist, is the very essence of sin. Ask the people of Noah's day how that turned out.

After the salmon spawns it dies. Their decaying bodies nourish the river and estuaries of their environment. Once a man discovers his place of origin and bends his knees to the One who created him, he dies a glorious death. Paul wrote, "I am crucified with Christ, nevertheless I live."[160] Faith in the true source of life puts to death all other empty pursuits. The man or woman who has placed their faith in Christ has died to self. A new foundation of life has been discovered bringing death to all other quests. Experiencing co-crucifixion with Christ, a new life emerges nourishing all his relationships. As Augustine once said, "the soul is restless until it finds its rest in God."[161] Source always determines destiny, and the source of man is the living God. The purpose of God's revelation to mankind is to reveal the utter futility and emptiness of any attempt to live life without him.

⊙⟋⟋⟍⟍⊙

I am the Alpha and the Omega, the first and the last, the beginning and the end. Blessed are those who wash their robes, so that they may have the right to the tree of life and that they may enter the city by the gates.

REVELATION 22:13,14 ESV

CHAPTER 35

A Dog's Day

Sometimes it's just a dog's day. Karen and I were recently sitting on our back porch, enjoying a cup of coffee, when we heard a rustling in the trees. Cooper, our Jack Russell Terrier, immediately leaped into action racing toward the disturbance in the branches. As he arrived, the two squirrels, who had been causing the ruckus, fell from the tree and landed at his feet. Talk about a lucky break. I can't recall ever seeing one of those fuzzy creatures fall off a branch much less two at a time. Cooper had finally reached his utopia. Fortunately, the squirrels were both faster than our dog. But oh, the joy he experienced in the chase. It was his day.

There are days like that for all of us. They are few and far between, but they do come, and it is usually right when we need them. God is good like that. He is keenly aware of every circumstance we face as he watches over our lives. He knows when we need a hug. God sees the finish line, and he knows when to give us a gust of wind to our backs to spur us on to the checkered flag. "For I know the thoughts that I think toward you, saith the LORD, thoughts of peace, and not of evil, to give you an expected end."[162] He rejoices in bringing us to the place of total dependance on him. This alone brings us joy.

Our son John called the other day to tell us of a recent dream he had experienced. It was about his grandfather who has been in Heaven for many years. They walked around his Pop's backyard and talked about the old days. John told him about his family. His Pop told him that Heaven was a thousand times better than he had ever imagined it to be. Now you may question in your mind if that was a dream God gave him, but I prefer to let it be what it was: a moment that encouraged our son to march on to the high calling of Jesus Christ. We've all had those moments that seemed to come out of nowhere to lift your spirits. We can't explain them, and I don't think we're supposed to try. They are meant to encourage us to march on to that heavenly city.

As wonderful as those days and moments seem to be, the fact that they seldom come should tell us something. Those special times are not the bread and butter of life. They are encouraging but we need a footing more secure and constant. I would suggest that the days in which we receive those, *hugs from the Lord*, are really our weakest times when we have allowed doubt to enter our hearts. Down and discouraged, the Lord lifts our head and in mysterious ways reminds us that we are loved. But again, this is not the norm in his dealings with us because there is a deeper and more abiding way called faith.

We walk by faith, not by sight, and so, our faith needs nothing from the world we live in to operate. "Faith is the substance of things hoped for, the evidence of things unseen."[163] To believe the promises of God when everything around us tells a different story sets our feet on a firmer foundation than those momentary blessings. His promises are enough. We have but to look to the Lord for the strength we need to face the next few minutes. "Look unto me, and be saved, all the ends of the earth: for I am God, and there is no one else."[164] The saving occurs the moment we "look" unto him.

The apostle John was a young man when Jesus called him, and he was an old man when he was sent to the island of Patmos for preaching the gospel. Much transpired between those two intervals, but one thing remained constant, John stayed faithful to Christ. It is estimated that John was in his 90s when he was imprisoned on the island for preaching the gospel. It is a wonderful thought that a man that old was still causing enough of a stir to be taken prisoner by the Romans. There was no slowing down for the old man who had once placed his head on the chest of Jesus at the Last Supper. Patmos, at that time, was nothing more than a rock in the Aegean Sea. It was an island where the Romans sent prisoners into exile. There were no retirement villas dotting the seaside and no assisted living accommodations with a view of the Mediterranean Sea. Rock quarrels and damp caves were the lot given to the man who had given his life for the

Savior. However, John was rewarded by God for the hateful treatment he received at the hands of the Romans. He received the revelation of Jesus Christ. He got the ultimate "dog's day," while sitting in a cave on a small island in the middle of nowhere.

This world can seem very dark at times. The dust that arises from the arena of conflict can become thick, threatening to choke us to death. Our enemy can appear imposing when we lose sight of the Victor of Heaven. It is easy to get pulled into a dark place where we forget the promise of his presence and his return. Decide today to face the future with faith in a God that loves you. Greater storms are coming my friend, but the Lord is our shelter when the gales blow. He will never forsake us even though we are tempted to believe that he has exited stage left. Never forget there is an all-powerful Son behind those clouds and with one blow from his breath, all troubles and trials will cease.

God grants us those "dog days" to remind us of his presence and what we can look forward to in Heaven. This world does not recognize us, but very soon their eyes will be opened to the fact that we are the children of God. In the same way that they did not know Jesus, when he walked on earth, they will not know us. "This is the age of humiliation for the saints, just as it was the age of humiliation for our Lord when he was on the earth..."[165] Paul writes in Romans, "For I consider that the sufferings of this present time are not worth comparing with the glory that is to be revealed in us. For the creation waits with eager longing for the revealing of the sons of God."[166] It is true that every dog has his day. Our day is fast approaching when we will see the One who is coming for us in the clouds. The apostle John, in the blackest of situations, had his day, and so shall we. Until then, keep your eye on the open gate and not on the dog catcher.

For I consider that the sufferings of this present time are not worth comparing with the glory that is to be revealed to us.

ROMANS 8:18 ESV

CHAPTER 36

Wasting Time

John Bunyan spent twelve years in an English prison for preaching the gospel. During that time, he wrote one of the greatest Christian allegories ever penned. Its original title was, *The Pilgrims Progress from this World to the World that is to Come.* First published in 1678, Bunyan's allegory of the Christian life has strengthened the hearts of believers ever since. The main character of the story is a young man named Christian. Encouraged by a spiritual guide named Evangelist, he is told he must leave the City of Destruction and journey to Mt Zion. After unsuccessfully attempting to bring his family along, the young man sets out on his quest of salvation. Along the path he meets Worldly Wisdom, falls into the Slough of Despond, and eventually ends up in the home of Interpreter who teaches him many lessons about faith. John Bunyan did an amazing job in describing the pitfalls and path of the Christian in this world.

In the end, John Bunyan's twelve years in the Bedford County Jail were not wasted. Rather than becoming absorbed in self-pity, Bunyan made good use of his time. No doubt, he would have preferred ministering from the comfort of his home and pulpit. Regardless, he used the time and circumstances God gave to glorify his Savior.

Given the choice between wasting time or money, I would rather waste the green stuff. We can make more money, but it is impossible to

MJ Gaylor

recoup time. There is only so much of it, and when it is gone, it is gone forever. When we speak of wasting time, it is really the fear of misusing of the hours God has given that is in view. It is how we spend our time that is the determining factor in judging our use of a day. When the clock strikes midnight, there is no rewind button we can push to get a second chance. We are all walking a path in life and each step is important. We want to know that when we get to the end, the journey has been worth the effort. A mouse on a treadmill exerts of a lot of energy but never really accomplishes anything of significance. It is important that we take time to think through these considerations before we busy ourselves into a frenzy. The sand in the hourglass of life is running out. As we look out over the coming days and years, there is a way we can be sure that we are not wasting our time with meaningless pursuits.

In his short, but powerful book, *The Tyranny of the Urgent*, Charles Hummel asks the following question, "Have you ever wished for a thirty-hour day? Surely this extra time would relieve the tremendous pressure under which we live. Our lives leave a trail of unfinished tasks. Unanswered letters, unvisited friends, unread books haunt quiet moments when we stop to evaluate what we have accomplished. We desperately need relief."[167] He then suggests a different approach to living after the model of Jesus' ministry. Hummel observed that at the end of Jesus' short life, he made the astonishing claim of having finished all that his Father had given him to accomplish. When you consider it, there were many in Israel who had not yet encountered Jesus. Countless lepers lay in misery, suffering continued for many, and yet, the Great Healer confidently claimed to have finished his ministry. How could this be? It appears he left so much undone. Certainly, he could have spoken a word and relieved the heartache and suffering of the entire world of his day. To do any less, would seem negligent.

In his earthly life, Jesus chose to limit himself by time and space. The geographical scope of his life's work was quite small. Jesus never traveled to any land outside of Israel except for a few trips into lands north of Galilee. Rather than healing everyone he encountered, he only touched those who had faith. In his own hometown of Nazareth, he could do no mighty works because they did not believe.[168] Even though much seemed to be unfinished, we must remember why Jesus came. His mission was to die for our sins and thus rescue us from an eternity in a lake of fire. Jesus came to redeem our souls, so that we could spend an eternity in Heaven with him. This task, he accomplished.

As he arose each day, he did not thumb through his daily planner to know what chores to accomplish. Hummel writes, "His life was never feverish; he had time for people. He could spend hours talking to one person, such as the Samaritan woman at the well. His life showed a wonderful balance, a sense of timing."[169] Jesus was in a constant attitude of prayer and fellowship with his Father, and as a result, he knew exactly what to do each moment of the day. He trusted his Father to guide his steps. Jesus purposefully left much undone, but in the end, he accomplished his mission. He died for all mankind, leaving the blessing of eternal salvation open to all who would come to him. He finished his work on earth. We all have a work to do on this earth, and the only way to finish it is by listening carefully to God's voice each day.

Paul reminded the churches in Crete to be careful to maintain good works.[170] I wish he had given us a list of good works to check off, but he didn't. Instead, Paul points to our faith in God as a means of knowing the good works he wants us to accomplish. He uses the word *maintain* as the muscle of the matter. Just as Jesus did, by looking to his Father, we can know each day what needs to be done and what needs to be left undone. By maintaining a steady gaze toward Christ each day, the Father works his will in our lives.

Life is a series of choices played out on the stage of life. The curtain rises with the morning sun and falls when the stars come out. Each performance lasts twenty-four hours, and we get only one chance to, *break a leg*. When the final whistle blows, there are no overtime periods. Our choices and energies must be all left on the field. Where shall I go today? What should I get done? As much as we try, we cannot check off everything we desire to accomplish in a day. Our list is as long as our arm, and we only have a pinky finger of time.

So, throw the list away and quietly listen for his voice. It is exciting to watch the Father patch together our days with people passing across our path. We get much more accomplished in the courts of Heaven when we choose to trust in his ordering of our days. Martha thought Mary was wasting her time at the feet of Jesus. What men consider waste is gold in

Heaven. Let me encourage you to be at peace with leaving things undone this day. The most important thing we accomplish each day is fellowship with Jesus. If we have spent time with him that is sufficient for the day's work. The only thing we really must do each day is set our hearts on Jesus.

⌒⫘⌒

This thing is trustworthy, and I want you to insist on these things so that those who have believed in God may be careful to devote themselves to good works.

TITUS 3:8 ESV

CHAPTER 37

The Unforgivable Sin

The need of forgiveness is universal because the calamity that calls out to it is universal; we all sin. I was a young boy, playing pitch and catch in my front yard, when my mother passed by on her way to work. I threw the baseball, and it struck her shin with a thud. Her face instantly revealed her pain and filled me with fear. My alarm was well founded as she marched over to me and knocked me to the ground with her large purse. I fully deserved every bit of her retribution. Lying there in the grass, I watched her march off to work. The side of my face stung, but what upset me most was that I had hurt my mother. The next time I saw her was the following day when she spotted me in the corner of the dining room with my head held down. I could barely lift my eyes to look at her for the shame I felt. What happened next changed everything. My mother walked over to me, lifted my face with her hands and said, "I forgive you, let's be friends." The need to be forgiven is so vital to our emotional well-being that the thought of an unforgivable sin is terrifying.

In one of Jesus' interactions with the religious leaders of his day he told them that there was a sin that could never be forgiven. He said, "And everyone who speaks a word against the Son of Man will be forgiven, but the one who blasphemes against the Holy Spirit will not be forgiven."[171] This statement was the direst warning to ever fall from the lips of the Master and has been the source of a raging debate for centuries. What is the unforgivable sin? Before we wrestle with this very important question, it is vital to know the true identity of Jesus Christ. If God alone can forgive sin, how could he make such a statement? Did he have the authority to declare that there is a sin that could never be forgiven? Let's further explore this question.

There is no topic in life more important than the destiny of the human soul. Where a man or woman will spend eternity carries with it everlasting bliss or terrifying misery. So vital is this subject that we cannot rely on the opinions of men. We must learn the truth concerning life after death from someone with the authority of God Himself. Fortunately, we have such a one. Jesus claimed to be God, and if this is true, then the weight of all he taught carries immense importance regarding the afterlife. If he is God, then his voice on the topic of Heaven and Hell silences all others and calls us into the realm of accountability. If Jesus is the God-Man, then he has the final word regarding our eternal destiny.

In the writings of C. S. Lewis, he suggested that Jesus was either a liar, a lunatic, or he is Lord! "A man who was merely a man and said the sort of things Jesus said would not be a great moral teacher. He would either be a lunatic — on the level with the man who says he is a poached egg — or else he would be the Devil of Hell."[172] By the process of elimination, Lewis narrows the choices down to the inevitable fact that Jesus is Lord. To disregard the fact that God walked this earth in the person of Jesus Christ is to risk eternal damnation in a lake of fire. To simply discount his words and his life, pushing them out to the margins, will come back to haunt us. Jesus alone taught the truth about his Father in Heaven, and his words are life to those who believe and condemnation to those who reject them.

It is important that we address the context of this statement to understand what Jesus was saying. He had just healed a man who was both blind and mute in the presence of the religious leaders. The man was also demon possessed. As the common people rejoiced, the Scribes and Pharisees went on the attack, accusing Jesus of using Satan's power to set the man free. Jesus countered their accusation with five separate arguments and then uttered his dire warning. He declared that to sin against the Holy Spirit would be unforgivable in this life and the life to come. A man can speak a word against the Son of God, Jesus said, and that would be forgiven, but not against the Holy Spirit. We have established the context, but we need to go further. To understand this teaching in its fullness we must dig deeper.

In speaking of the Holy Spirit's arrival at Pentecost, Jesus taught that he would fulfill three distinct purposes in the world.[173] First, to those who had not yet believed, the Spirit would convict of sin. It is the work of the Holy Spirit to show a man that he is a sinner. The Lord told Paul on the road to Damascus that it was hard to kick against the gourds. Gourds were sharp poles that the oxen driver used to steer his cattle down a certain path. The Holy Spirit was bearing down on Paul, and as a result, the young man was becoming increasingly uncomfortable. Notice it was hard to resist, but not impossible. A man can repel the prompting of the Spirit because God will not violate man's free will. Paul was struggling with guilt because the Spirit was casting light on his sin.

Furthermore, the Spirit would convince believers of his righteousness now bestowed. The Holy Spirit would impress upon the heart of his disciples that they were fully forgiven and free from the power of sin over their lives. Lastly, the fact that the Spirit came down was evidence that Satan had been defeated paving the way for all men to be saved. Our present study concerns the first purpose, namely the Holy Spirit's responsibility to convict men of their sin. He does this in a very specific way.

When the Spirit begins his probing work, he does not bring a long list of accusations to the table against a man. Jesus said there is only one unforgivable sin. He does not name every sin we have committed and then work backwards from that point; he goes for the taproot. His focus is on the sin of unbelief. Before unredeemed man can be saved, he must believe in the testimony of the Holy Spirit concerning the gospel of Jesus Christ. Jesus said when the Holy Spirit comes, he will speak of me.[174] It is Jesus Christ who is being pressed upon the soul when the Holy Spirit is doing his convicting work. The unforgivable sin is resisting what the Spirit is revealing concerning Christ's death, burial, and resurrection. In the same way that the Jewish leadership was attributing the healing of the demoniac to Satan, man can reject the testimony of the Holy Spirit concerning Christ. It is counting the work of Christ as nothing. Turning away from the offer of eternal life is the only sin that can never be forgiven. Men remain eternally in darkness by rejecting the light.

When I played football, I would occasionally run the ball. Mostly,

I was running for my life. I soon discovered that my best friend while carrying the old pigskin was something called a stiff-arm. In football you are not allowed to punch the opposing player, but you are permitted to hold your arm out stiff and repel your would-be tackler. What worked well on a football field will send a man to hell. The only sin that is unforgivable, is stiff-arming the Holy Spirit when he presents a man an opportunity to come to Christ. If you are still breathing and are fretful that you have committed this sin, you have not. Push away fear and run to Jesus. Today, if you hear his voice, do not harden your hearts.[175] You see, the man who was blind and mute could still hear quite well. God made sure of it. Mankind will have no excuse. When you hear the Spirit calling, listen, and receive him as your Lord and Savior.

⌘

Therefore, I tell you every sin and blasphemy
will be forgiven people, but the blasphemy
against the Spirit will not be forgiven.

MATTHEW 12:31 ESV

CHAPTER 38

Aunt Minnie

W hen I was a lad, my parents took me to visit Aunt Minnie. She was 100 years old. I remember her sitting in a chair holding a peanut butter sandwich in her old, wrinkled hand. She was a little lady with no teeth, and so, she sat there gumming her sandwich as though it were her last meal on earth. Aunt Minnie grinned slightly as she kept repeating, "I like peanut butter." Her voice carried a passion for peanut butter that I could appreciate. We were only there for a few moments, but I remember the scene and only recently understood how special that moment was for me. Many years later, while looking at an old family photograph, I spotted her. The year was 1888, and Minnie Saxton was twenty years old. Quickly doing the math I realized she was born just after the end of the Civil War.

In meeting Aunt Minnie, I was privileged to look into the face of one who had been born during a difficult time in our nation's history. As a young boy, I failed to appreciate the moment, but my parents understood the importance of exposing me to my personal family history. On a grander scale, I realized I am a part of a legacy of humanity stretching back thousands of years in a family that has touched every point of human history. We are not isolated generations unaffected by all that went before us, and our lives will touch future generations. More importantly, my life and the decisions I make spiritually will powerfully impact my posterity.

My parents understood the importance of dragging a nine-year-old boy along for the ride. They were investing in my future by sharing the moments that mattered.

On the contrary, the disciples of Jesus viewed the children that were brought to him as a nuisance. Their parents were not being respectful of the Master's time, they surmised. After all, Jesus was an up-and-coming rabbi, a man of great importance. The little ones, gathering around his feet, contributed nothing to his ministry, and were, in fact, hindering him. Those children, they concluded, would never know the significance of being in the presence of Jesus. The disciples meant well, but they were wrong. The Lord, observing their attitude, rebuked them sharply. "Let the little children come to me and do not hinder them, for such belongs the kingdom of Heaven."[176] What the disciples saw as a waste of time, Jesus considered something of eternal value. Looking into their eyes, he saw those who would inhabit his kingdom.

There are some who would argue that the children Jesus touched and prayed over were clueless to the significance of their encounter with him. However, the great impact that it had later in their lives was no doubt enormous. Imagine being in the early church, as a follower of Jesus, and knowing that you once sat on the Son of God's lap and were held by him in your infancy or childhood. How grateful you would have been to be given that distinction.

The impact those parents made when they brought their children to Jesus took root later in their lives. Did they remember the press of his kiss on their cheek? Maybe. Did they marvel when the story was told, years later, that Jesus loved them and had embraced them? Yes! People who value children understand their own mortality and the importance of leaving behind a legacy of faith and hope. Our children are watching our lives and looking for a real faith that makes a difference in how we live. It may not appear as though taking them to church makes any impact on their lives, but it does far greater good than you can imagine. My father-in-law recalled his mother gathering he and his siblings each night to tell them stories from the Bible. Even in his old age tears would fill his eyes as he remembered those special memories. His mother understood that she was planting seeds that we may never see come to fruition. She was deeply impacting his life with the gospel. Wise is the mother who understands the blessing and power of motherhood. In the Old Testament, Hannah was such a woman; she only needed the opportunity by being blessed with a baby.

Hannah was childless, and her heart was broken. She pleaded with the Lord and fussed with her husband, Elkanah, but to no avail. His other wife produced child after child, which only made the situation more painful. On one of their yearly pilgrimages to Shiloh, she was observed while in prayer. She promised the Lord that if he blessed her with a son, she would bring the child up in the fear of the Lord. She further vowed that the child would be given to the Lord to serve in his house. Thinking she was drunk, Eli rebuked her.[177] Rather than encourage her prayer, Eli's thoughts had grown dark and evil toward God's people. The old prophet had grown sloppy in ministry, and the Lord was going to use the fruit of Hannah's womb to replace him. Finally, she became pregnant and gave birth to Samuel.

As a young boy, Samuel no doubt heard the story of his mother's prayer many times. Her commitment to give him back to God was the foundation of the young boy's life. God used Eli to raise the boy in the temple for the purpose of replacing him. God often uses the younger generation to clear the stagnant air of religion and usher in a freshness of life that has been clouded by the dullness of old men. However, there is another angle to the story of the Master's blessing of the children.

When the parents brought their children to Jesus, no one, including the disciples, understood the significance of that moment in Jesus's life. He was at the end of his earthly ministry. The Savior had been rejected by the Jewish authorities, ignored by Rome, and misunderstood by the multitudes. The disciples themselves seemed clueless as to the reason he came. But most significantly, he was only days away from facing his death on the cross. The intensity of the pressure on him in those last stages of his ministry was enormous. Instead of returning to Heaven on the Mount of Transfiguration, he had walked down that hillside and faced a demon-possessed man. Undeterred, he journeyed to Jerusalem to face an arrest, a trial, and a cruel death. It was during this struggle that the children were brought to him. It is a beautiful thought that Jesus took them up in his arms. Perhaps, this was a moment that he needed to be reminded of why he had come to die for mankind. There is nothing so simple and beautiful as the faith of a child. As he looked into their eyes, is it possible that the struggle was eased, and his burden lifted a bit? The simplicity of their trustful eyes cheered him.

We don't know why those parents brought their children to Jesus, but their decision to do so blessed their lives. Those innocent little ones also encouraged Jesus in a moment when he desperately needed it. Parents, grandparents, keep bringing your little ones to Jesus. I was blessed for having met Minnie Saxton. I look forward to seeing her in Heaven and sharing a peanut butter sandwich.

ᕲᨒᨒᨒᕲ

Then children were brought to him that he might lay his hands on them and pray.

MATTHEW 19:13 ESV

CHAPTER 39

A Late Bloomer

It was psychoanalyst Elliot Jaques who first coined the term *midlife crisis* in 1965. Best understood, it is a person's recognition of their own mortality. A midlife crisis begins when we realize there's a whole lot less road ahead than behind. The sides of our casket are closing in, and there is little we can do to avoid the velvet walls. We hear the roar of the waterfall just around the bend and know that we have no other choice but to fall over it into the chasm below. It is a boxed-in feeling, a sense of inevitable breathlessness. We begin to say things like, "I hope to have twenty good years left," or, "If my health stays good..." The thought occurred to me recently that in ten years, my daughter could be a grandmother. If there is any silver lining to all of this, it is the fact that we are living longer today, which makes a midlife crisis even possible. In any regard, the end is coming, and we know time is short.

In examining my own life, I have always been a late bloomer, and so, I have waited until the ripe old age of sixty to enter my own mid-life crisis. Not that we can chart the average age of such things, but I was expecting it a few years ago. Better late than never I suppose. So far, my symptoms have been mild. A few foolish purchases from Amazon and my desire for a flock of chickens have been the worst of it. Now, just so you young whippersnappers don't get all uppity, if you live long enough, you will run into the same speed bump. Someday you will mention Justin Bieber, and your grandchildren will think you just named a new animal species. The joints and bones you take for granted now will turn on you. Your tight skin will suddenly become wrinkly, and gravity will be your greatest enemy. You have been warned.

Unfortunately, the bad news gets worse. The writer of Ecclesiastes tells us that no one will remember us when we are gone. Solomon wrote, "And I said in my heart that this also is vanity. For of the wise as of the fool, there is no enduring remembrance seeing that in the days to come all will have been long forgotten."[178] I recently mentioned Frank Sinatra before our congregation, and all the young people gave me a blank look. Mark it down, if they don't remember Frank, they won't remember you. All that we accomplish will be like dust in the wind. There's another reference you will not get unless you grew up in the 70s. All our achievements will fade away. When the next crop of youthful renegades appears on the scene, they will see us as archaic monuments to a time long ago. I was recently asked by one of my grandchildren if we had electricity when I was growing up. Kick up all the sand you can, and it will settle back onto the beach and be washed away with the outgoing tide. What is left of our sand sculptures will be knocked over by a toddler racing down the shoreline. Before we are cold in the grave, the beach will be loaded with new sandcastles.

Although these thoughts seem discouraging, there are certain benefits to growing older. The realization that we only have so much time left causes our plans going forward to become precise and calculated. We understand that wasting time and energy on foolish endeavors is a game for those who think the end will never come. Today, we must say what needs to be said and do what needs to be done. Procrastination is the luxury of youth. We also tend to be overlooked, which is a wonderful place to be. All the pressure to perform is gone. Once we reach that golden age, we are set free from the expectations of other people. The generation that is coming on the scene just wants us to be quiet and happy. I have learned that by maintaining a tired face while they visit, helps to keep the illusion alive that I should be left alone to eat my Jell-O and take my Meta-Mucil. Once they leave, I wash my face and get back at it. Expectations lowered; mission accomplished. Rather than discouraging, this truth frees us to wander off in new directions. We finally have the time for new adventures and fresh battles. I have also discovered that God is not done using us old fogies.

When we investigate the Bible, old warriors abound. Moses was a ripe eighty years old when he went down into Egypt to deliver the Jewish nation. Noah had full-grown children when God interrupted his humble life to build an ark. Sampson wasn't a spring chicken when he turned the Philistines temple into rubble. In his death, he killed more of his enemies than he did in his life. The apostle John was in his 90's when he experienced a vision of the end times and wrote the book of Revelation.

However, in my opinion, the greatest example of a successful late bloomer was a man named Caleb. He was a youthful forty-year-old when chosen to be one of the spies that first entered the Promise Land. He then had to wait forty more years in the wilderness wanderings to claim the land he saw during the expedition of Canaan. At eighty-five years old, he told Joshua that he wanted the hill country of Hebron where fortified cities and giants lived. Caleb insisted he still possessed the strength of his younger days, and he knew God would drive the Anakim out of those stone cities. No one else wanted to fight those giants. When other old men were slurping smoothies and watching Jeopardy, Caleb wanted to climb mountains and take down giants. He still had the drive and ambition to find new adventures. No retirement home for that old man. He wanted everything God had promised. This man refused to wallow about in the glories of how life use to be while bemoaning his aching joints. He wanted to go out swinging and kicking. As a result, God granted his desire. Caleb conquered the Anakim and stood on that mountain in victory. He went out in a blaze of glory.

My father once told me that those who live in the past have no future. Good words. If we have twenty more good years, then let them be the best twenty years of our lives. Regardless of our health, let us walk confidently through each day. May we choose not to rush through life and miss the important moments and the people God wants us to influence. Let's slow down, enjoy every day, and drink in every second of life.

There is one more point to be made, and it is the grandest thought of all. At the end of this short life, lays an eternity of endless bliss for those who know Christ. The seventy or eighty years we rustle about on this spinning globe are only the prologue to a never-ending story. So, take heart my fellow old-timers, we are just getting started. There is much that we can teach the younger generation if they will listen. If they aren't listening, just remember the best advice comes from a place of active living. Meanwhile, I think I'll go shopping for a few good hens and a rooster.

⌀⫘⌀

All go to one place. All are from the
dust, and to dust all return.

ECCLESIASTES 3:20 ESV

CHAPTER 40

The Hope That Endures

ope means many things to many people. Usually when we think of hope, our aspirations come to mind and the dreams we have yet to fulfill. The word hope can be used for something far off like a new home built in the country or as short-lived as hoping tomorrow will bring a brighter day. Hope fills us with happiness when the world seems right and evaporates when life becomes sour. Hope is fickle. It surges through us one moment and then floats away like a balloon released from a child's tiny fingers. Hope never rests. Once we achieve our dreams, it sets sail for the next buried treasure. The next great adventure keeps us moving forward.

However, regardless of whatever form it takes and whatever situation it finds itself in, hope is always reaching for what it does not possess. "Now hope that is seen is not hope. For who hopes for what he sees? But if we hope for what we do not see, we wait for it with patience."[179] Hope is always striving for the best outcomes. The Bible talks much about hope but in a very different way. Rather than setting our sights on something in the future, biblical hope looks backward to a promise made by God that is yet unfulfilled. It claims that our destiny is based on a promise from the One who cannot fail. The Scripture refers to hope as an anchor for the soul. For example, Jesus promised that he would return one day, which is what the Bible calls, *The Blessed Hope.*[180] We look to the skies with a confident expectation. This is the brick and mortar of biblical faith.

Recently, I visited a dear lady in Hospice, who only had a few days to live. As I looked into her weak eyes, I saw a life worn thin with cancer. I quickly realized that our conversation would be one sided. Sitting down next to her, I held her hand and fumbled for a topic. What could I say to lift her spirits and calm her fears? The newest building project at the church seemed silly since she would never live to see it. The latest political developments were certainly a waste of time as well as the current societal changes the world was experiencing. The Lord was soon to set her free from all these concerns. She had stopped eating days ago, so a question concerning the quality of food served at the Hospice was also meaningless. In that moment, the only topic that came to mind was how much Jesus loved her. I assured her that better days were ahead, and soon she would be loose of the cords binding her to this earth and free from her present pain. I spoke of the heavenly city she would soon enter and the loved ones she would meet again. My desire was to give her hope, real hope. After a brief time, I prayed with her and left.

As I pushed open the doors and breathed fresher air, the thought occurred to me that the only message that really matters in this life is Jesus. All else fades into obscurity when life boils down to its most common denominator. Life becomes quite simple when faced with death. When our heartbeat slows, and our breath is fleeting, the only worthy topic is Jesus. He is the hope that anchors the soul. My friend needed hope but not the kind the world offers. She needed the hope which looks back to the promises of God, not a hope that something good might happen. She was trusting in the One who is always faithful. "For I know whom I have believed, and I am convinced that he is able to guard until that day what has been entrusted to me."[181] Biblical hope is confidence in the promises of God; that what he promised, he would fulfill. Jesus promised that he would give us a kingdom and he will not fail. He assured us that all things work together for good to those who love God. He told his disciples that their reward in Heaven would be great.

In the book of Revelation, the church at Smyrna was facing intense persecution. In a city that was described as the crown of Asia for its beauty, this church was promised a different crown, an eternal reward. Poverty was their lot and death by persecution was their immediate future. Instead of rescuing them, which he could have easily done, Jesus reminded them of their eternal future. The hope he gave them was an anchor amid the storm. His promise of a glorious reward was their expectation. "Do not fear what you are about to suffer. Behold, the devil is about to throw some of you into prison, that you may be tested, and for ten days you will have tribulation. Be faithful unto death, and I will give you the crown of life."[182] With the uncertainty of life, we all need a steady rock by which to anchor our lives.

Consider the following story. Gliding over Crystal Lake, my friend and I looked over the side of our boat to see the bottom some forty feet down. The water was so clear it could have been a hundred feet deep, and we still would have made out every detail of the lake floor. After finding our favorite fishing spot, my friend made his way to the front of our little boat and grabbed the anchor. As he lowered the heavy hook, he spotted the same large, jagged rock, named Old Sally, that we had used since our younger days. In other lakes, we had to search a muddy bottom to find something to anchor us, but in contrast, the clear water of Crystal Lake and Old Sally never failed us. Once the anchor found the lip of the rock, we knew we were secure. We fished there for hours without the boat drifting away. The purity of the lake water and faithful Old Sally never disappointed us.

In contrast to the muddy lakes of this world, where it is difficult to find anything to which we can anchor our lives, the water of the Word of God is pure, and the rock of Truth is strong and secure. The hope that endures is found in his promises, and we discover that Jesus is our steady hope. He is our shelter in the storms of life. God said, "I will never leave you or forsake you."[183] We don't need sermons that encourages us to live on the sunny side of life or to pray till we get our breakthrough. Our breakthrough occurred two thousand years ago when Jesus paid the price for our sins. We need the assurance that this life is only the beginning of our journey and that a glorious future awaits us.

As I drove off that day, I knew that the next time I would see my friend was in Heaven. I was reminded of the promise that Jesus loves us and will never leave us. A few weeks later I preached her funeral. There, in the crowd, were many of her friends and loved ones who did not know Christ. Her death provided the opportunity to share the hope of the gospel to men and women who needed to hear it.

In this present life, there are so many things beyond our control. Nevertheless, our confidence lies in the fact that he is in control. His choices for our lives as painful as they can be, are always perfect. The Lord never makes a mistake, and whatever we encounter in this life just makes Heaven sweeter. "For I know the plans I have for you, declares the LORD, plans for peace and not for evil, to give you a future and a hope."[184] The burdens of life impact us all. Circumstances arise to drag our minds into despair. Days that begin with the promise of sunshine end with the storm clouds of discouragement. We have all experienced times when the return of Jesus sounded like music in our ears. What is the answer to the heaviness of life? How do we endure the dark days of Hospice? We must rest in the hope that what he has promised he will accomplish. The only hope for our dry and dusty lives is the presence of Jesus Christ and our eternal future in Heaven.

I will never leave you nor forsake you.

HEBREWS 13:5 KJV

CHAPTER 41

Raising Good Kids

The term, an open secret, is an oxymoron. Like jumbo shrimp or fresh frozen fruit, the phrase combines two opposing words that do not negate each other. Webster defines an open secret as, "a supposedly secret but generally known matter."[185] One of the great *open secrets* of our culture is what it takes to be a good parent. Good parenting is not some dark mystery hidden away in the dusty books of a psychology department. The path to success is full of good old fashion horse sense. Most parents know instinctively how to raise children that are a blessing to them. In most cases, they just lack the courage and will.

Raising good kids is not rocket science. Even animals in the wild know how to train their young. Have you ever seen an eagle push its young out of the nest to teach it to fly? Many animals teach their young to hunt. Now, before I get on my soap box, let me define *good kids*. They are not perfect kids. Good kids are the ones who the kindergarten teachers love to have in their class. They sit down when they are told, raise their hands before speaking and interact well with others. They are respectful to adults and their peers. Good kids are quiet when they are told to be and play like wild Comanches when free to do so. They clean up after themselves and take responsibility for their actions. Notice, nothing was mentioned about intelligence, athletic ability, or talent. It is always character that counts, and character can be instilled in any child; it just takes a lot of work.

Hopefully, at this point, you haven't thrown your chips in and thought that it's impossible to raise a child like that. I beg to differ. I have witnessed the phenomenon firsthand. My opening statement in this paragraph rings true, raising good kids is not rocket science. However, there is one major obstacle to overcome, and most parents get blindsided by it. It all goes back to what happened in the Garden of Eden.

When God created Adam and Eve, his desire was for them to have dominion over his creation. However, this could only be realized after *they* accepted God's dominion over their lives, which they rejected. By refusing God's dominion, they utterly failed to fulfill their destiny. Sin entered humanity, and one of its distinguishing marks was man's desire to have dominion over others. It is this singular, driving passion that defines sinful behavior, and it abides in the heart of every child born into every home. That little innocent looking baby, resting in its bassinet, is plotting your downfall. He or she is a mini narcissist who is looking forward to the day when dominion over you can be accomplished. It is your primary job as a parent to prevent this from occurring. The first responsibility of every parent is to understand that what they have on their hands is a little sinner. Behind that tiny smile is the desire for global domination, and that begins by pulling your strings at every turn. Effective parenting does not begin until that realization dawns on the heart of mom and dad. Someone is going to end up being king of the hill, and it must be you.

If you push aside the psychological mumbo jumbo, there are only two essential elements in the job description. As parents, we all make a thousand mistakes, but if these two steps are faithfully followed, then the chances of offering a functioning adult to society is greatly increased. Children need discipline and love. These two principles must be firmly rooted into the fiber of a child's life at a very young age. The earlier you start teaching these two values, the better. The clay is softest at a young age, and the first year is not early enough to begin to mold them. When a child knows that your word is law, and they are confident of your love, the foundation of all other teachings will be secure and strong. The balance of these two practical elements is the key to it all.

At the age of twelve, Jesus went with his parents to Jerusalem. In the mix of the crowd, they lost him and did not know it until they were out on the road leading north to Galilee. If you have ever lost a child in a crowd, you can imagine Mary's panic. In her case, it was even worst. She had misplaced God. When they found him, he was surprised at their bewilderment. "Why were you looking for me? Did you not know that I must be in my Father's house?"[186] What followed was an astonishing statement. "And he went down with them and came to Nazareth and was submissive to them."[187]

The parents of Jesus had done their job. The argument may be made that since Jesus was God, little parenting was needed, but the book of Hebrews tells us that he learned obedience by the things which he suffered. Of course, Jesus never had to be disciplined for wrongdoing, but he had been taught to be submissive to their authority and he knew they loved him.

Between the two components of love and discipline, the latter is of the greater importance. A child in the home must know who is in charge, and that parental respect is never to be questioned. If your child doesn't respect you, the possibility for a loving relationship is impossible. Now by discipline I don't mean harshness, I mean firmness. Children should obey your command the first time. Stop counting! Never repeat a clear command. Obedience is doing what they're told, when they're told, and with a good attitude. Never ignore a bad attitude, it is the seed bed of all bad behavior. A child should never ask a second time once they have been told no to a request. They should know that misbehavior brings swift discipline. Kids are not built to be in charge; you are. They are too immature to lead the pack. Their security lives inside strong boundaries put in place by committed, loving parents. Always settle for nothing less than full obedience always.

Secondly, love them unconditionally. Read to them. Play with them. Teach your kids to hit a ball or fly a kite. Discover what they are interested in and become interested with them. When they sin, forgive them once sorrow is acknowledged. Take the time to listen to them about their day; they have troubles too. Give them freedom to be a kid. They are going to be childish at times, so don't expect more than their age permits. Respect them and allow them to make choices, within limits, of course. Never expect two kids to be alike. Laugh with them, wrestle with them, and get down on the floor and act goofy with them. A famous diplomat once found Thomas Jefferson in the White House wrestling with his grandchildren on the floor.

While discipline and love are essentials to a child's development, there is a third factor that far outweighs them both in importance. The parents of Jesus brought him to worship in Jerusalem. This spoke volumes of their priorities. When parents walk intimately with Jesus Christ, the impact that this has on a child is enormous. Faithful attendance to church services communicates to a child that God is important enough to spend time in worship. When a young person sees their parents praying and discussing the Bible in the home, it leaves a lifelong impression. There is no substitute for vibrant spiritual lives, lived out before a child. Sunday school classes and church services can only do so much. If there is a contradictory life lived out before them at home, it undermines anything done at church. Timothy knew the Scriptures from a young child. Paul writes, "And how from childhood you have been acquainted with the sacred writings, which are able to make you wise for salvation through faith in Christ Jesus."[188] He reminded the young man of his sincere faith which was first seen in his grandmother Lois and his mother Eunice.

If all this sounds old fashion, it is, and the quicker parents discover that the old paths still work, the better. By the way, I didn't say it was easy; I said it wasn't rocket science. You'll make a multitude of mistakes, but if you give them healthy doses of discipline and love they'll turn out fine. If your walk with the Lord is authentic, they will follow your example. All kids make mistakes but, in the end, they may surprise you. As my father used to say, "I didn't raise any angels."

☙❧

Even a child makes himself known by his acts,
by whether his conduct is pure and upright.

PROVERBS 20:11 ESV

CHAPTER 42

Truth on the Throne

I have a sweet tooth the size of a woolly mammoth tusk. Glazed, dipped in caramel, or covered with powdered sugar, if it's sweet, it's for me. I will never forget the first time I bit into a piece of fried dough at the county fair. When Krispy Kreme doughnuts are being lifted out of the hot grease, and then baptized in that flowing river of white sugar, a shiver runs down my spine and my knees buckle. Chocolate cake with whip cream icing, yes please, and I would not be angry if you placed a scoop of ice cream next to it! However, what works well in the world of pies and pastries does not translate into the world of theology. There are some things that I do not want sugar-coated.

For instance, if my doctor discovers I have cancer, I do not want to be told to go home and take an aspirin. I want him or her to look me in the eye and tell me the truth. If my cholesterol is high, I need to know what foods to eat to bring it down. I want to be told the truth, because anything less is a betrayal of the trust that I have in my doctor. Even more importantly, my health is at risk. When my truck limps into the mechanic's shop, I do not want to be sold a set of tires when I need a new transmission. I also want my wife to be honest with me. We are sharing life together, and if I am causing her a bumpy ride, then I need to hear that, regardless of my feelings. We need all these people to shoot straight with us and tell us what we need to hear, not what we want to hear. If we create a barrier around ourselves that precludes anyone from telling us the truth, it will only spell our downfall. The last thing any of us need is a group of yes-men, bobbing their heads up and down and shielding us from painful truths. Sharp cuts are clean cuts that heal quickly.

Likewise, we need our preachers to tell us the truth. Sugar-coating the great dilemma of the human condition does nothing to cure the rebellion found within the heart of man. Telling us that the devil made us do it, rather than our own sinful nature, lets us off the hook. Glazing over the obvious fact of sin within, is like sprinkling powdered sugar over a pile of cattle dung. We need our pastor to open the Bible and preach the Word in an uncompromising manner. It is only when we face the cold, hard facts from God's estimation, that we can begin to grow as believers. We desperately need to listen to God's word, because it is the only way we will ever make progress toward freedom from the tyranny within ourselves. False preachers, with their shallow platitudes and pointless stories, will always betray our trust, and they have been around for thousands of years. Consider this story from the Old Testament.

In the book of First Kings, Israel and Judah were preparing to go to war against Syria. Ahab, at the request of Jehoshaphat, gathered 400 prophets to hear from the Lord concerning their military campaign. With one corporate cry, all the preachers lifted their voices to bless these two kings in their fight against Syria. Jehoshaphat was not satisfied. He could see through there shallow, insincere performance. "Is there not here another prophet of the Lord of whom we may inquire," he asked. Ahab's response was classic. "There was one left named Micaiah," Ahab replied. "But he always speaks evil of me."[189] Micaiah's mission was to tell the truth regardless of anyone's feelings and Ahab resented him for it.

Upon the insistence of Jehoshaphat, Micaiah was called. As the prophet entered the assembly, he was warned by a messenger to tow the party line. He was clearly instructed to say what the kings wanted to hear, and all will be well. Thankfully, he decided to stay faithful to God and his message. "As the LORD lives, what the LORD says to me, that I will speak," he answered.[190]

Standing before these two kings, he glanced over at the 400 preachers and shook his head. What a sad group of puppets, controlled by the strings of the kings, he thought. Micaiah decided to use sarcasm to get his message across as it seemed fitting for these men in their royal clothing and regalia. Oscar Wilde once called sarcasm the "lowest form of wit," which reveals what Micaiah thought of the intellectual prowess of the men who stood before him. And he answered him, "Go up and triumph; the LORD will give it into the hand of the king."[191] Annoyed by the preacher's obvious display of sarcasm, Jehoshaphat became angry. "How many times shall I make you swear that you speak to me nothing but the truth in the name of the LORD?"[192]

Afterwards, Micaiah plainly told the two kings that they would be unsuccessful in their fight against Syria. Destruction and death awaited them if they persisted in their plans. Ahab stomped about. "I told you he had nothing good to say concerning me."[193] Men who want nothing more than a rubber stamp on their willful plans detest preachers who speak the truth. They would rather suffer their self-inflicted wounds than listen to godly counsel, but one preacher who speaks truth is more powerful than four hundred who lie, and Ahab knew it.

Micaiah decided to turn to sarcasm once more as he told them of a supposed vision in Heaven. "The Lord sat on his throne before the host of Heaven," Micaiah begins. "And asked how shall we entice Ahab to go up to battle against Syria and be killed? Many suggestions poured in, until one stepped forward and suggested putting a lying spirit in the mouth of Ahab's prophets."[194] At this point Micaiah turns and faces the horde of false preachers and tells the kings, "Now therefore behold, the LORD has put a lying spirit in the mouth of all these your prophets; the LORD has declared disaster for you."[195] The prophet predicted the demise of both men.

Sadly, I would like to say these two rulers listened to the true prophet of God, but they did not. As two blind mice, led by the smell of rotten cheese, they went north into battle. Ahab was killed, and Jehoshaphat ran for his life. It would be a wonderful thing if all men responded to the truth of the gospel by bending their knees to Jesus Christ, but that is not reality. James Russel Lowell once famously wrote, "truth forever on the scaffold wrong forever on the throne."[196] He was wrong. Truth has always been on the throne; it just doesn't appear that way for now.

The apostle Paul warned in the last days men would gather to themselves preachers who would tell them what they wanted to hear. He described these men as having itching ears.[197] Preachers who compromise the gospel for the sake of drawing a big crowd and subsequently a big offering are as common as weeds in the garden. As soon as you pull one out of the ground, another appears to choke the good crops. For the sake of popularity, these men conveniently dance around hard truths. They replace the gospel with soft sayings, easy to be digested by those who have lost their stomach for truth.

With this wretched situation in mind, Paul wrote this concerning the end times, "And with all deceivableness of unrighteousness in them that perish; because they received not the love of the truth, that they might be saved. And for this cause God shall send them strong delusion, that they should believe a lie. That they all might be damned who believed not the truth but had pleasure in unrighteousness."[198] Oswald Chambers once said, "In other callings you have to work with men, but in this calling, you work upon men; you come with the authority men crave for and yet resent."[199] Sin, according to the Bible, is rebellion against God, and there is only one remedy for it: the cross of Christ. When we underestimate the power the sin, we fall to it every time. We will make a thousand excuses for our poor behavior until we are confronted by the truth of God's word.

All of us have a choice to make when we hear the doctor's negative report. We can reject it or believe it, but one thing is sure, our decision does not change the reality within the report.

We can reject God's estimation of our sin, but in doing so, we will continue down a path of destruction that leads to the eternal fires of hell. Before we can be forgiven, we must acknowledge that we are sinners and in need of a Savior. Before we can advance as believers, we must agree that "in our flesh dwells no good thing."[200] For those who receive God's word, what is difficult to swallow, becomes sweet to the soul.

⌀⟋

For all have sinned and fall short of the glory of God.

ROMANS 3:23 ESV

CHAPTER 43

Falling to New Heights

It is always tragic when someone loses everything they own. We spend a lifetime pursuing our dreams and never know when or if they will be taken away in a moment. The same rain that nourishes the earth can quickly become a flood, washing aside everything that is precious to us. It is even sadder when we trip over an obstacle that we ourselves have placed in our path. Through a careless, unguarded moment, we can light a fire that destroys relationships and quickly brings our downfall. By a regretful decision, we can cripple our ability to move on in life. There are circumstances in life that only God can rescue us from and thankfully, he comes to our aid. However, there are times when losing something we dearly possess can be the best thing for us. Falling from certain places in life can bring us to heights we never imagined.

In my rapidly declining years, I have discovered that I am falling more often. My sense of equilibrium has faltered, causing me to become dizzier on a ladder and wobblier as I climb out of bed. I've been instructed by my loved ones to stay off ladders, but as anyone knows, you can't get certain things done without climbing the rungs and ascending the heights. Trees do not prune themselves and gutters do not expel leaves naturally. Recently, while taking the shutters off my house, I began to fall backwards. Fortunately, my descent was from a six-foot ladder, but unfortunately it was over top of my shrubbery. In a split moment I had to make an important decision. Fight the fall and end up in the thorny bushes or leap into the air and aim for the grass. The latter decision was taken, and I sustained no serious injury other than my pride and a few grass stains.

As in any stage of life, it is important to learn certain things to survive, and since this tendency to fall has become a reality, I have decided to study its dynamics. In my research, I have discovered three vital truths concerning the art of falling. First, do not fight the fall. It is vital to relax during a rapid descent. If you hit the ground with your muscles tensed, the chance of injury increases. Secondly, look for a soft place to land. Grass is to be preferred over rosebushes. Soft dirt tends to cushion the blow, while asphalt will rip open your flesh. Finally, after you have landed, look around to make sure no one has seen you. If you have been observed, quickly offer money for their silence. If it is reported too many times that you have fallen, your family or friends will begin to look for an assisted living accommodation, and I am not quite ready for tapioca pudding and a nap. The apostle Peter learned that what is true of a physical fall applies to the spiritual realm as well.

When Peter entered the courtyard of the High Priest on the night of the Lord's trial, he had no idea he was in for the fall of his life. He was simply there in hope that he could rescue Jesus. After all, watching out for the Master was his job. Along with James and John, the big fisherman had been privy to the greatest miracles Jesus performed. He was in the room when Jesus raised a young girl from the dead. Peter had walked up the Mount of Transfiguration and seen the glorified Savior. It was he who suggested they all stay on that mountaintop instead of returning to deal with the messy humanity that was waiting for them down in the valley. Peter had become the unofficial, unelected leader of the apostolic band, and he felt its pressure.

Peter also possessed a strong personality, which remained a hindrance to himself and the others. Open mouth, insert foot was his mode of operandi. When Jesus spoke of his death, it was Peter who was determined to talk him out of it. The death of his leader was something he could not bear, and so, he spoke his mind. The man who would rebuke Jesus was rebuked himself with the most stringing pronouncement ever to roll off the lips of the Master. "Get behind me Satan! You are a hindrance to me. For you are not setting your mind on the things of God, but on the things of man."[201] In the garden, Peter had swung a sword, only to cut off an ear. He was humiliated and defeated before the other disciples as he dropped his weapon. Peter had failed in every attempt to be the leader of the other disciples. As Jesus was being arrested, Peter was determined to redeem himself by rescuing Jesus from the teeth of the lion. The proud, determined fisherman was ripe for a fall.

On that night, in the High Priest's house, Peter was confronted about being a follower of Jesus. He denied being a disciple of Jesus three times. As he sank lower and lower, all his courage left him. He was seized with a deep sense of weakness. Peter, larger than life, could not even stand strong before a young girl's inquiry at the gate. To make matters worse, young John was there listening to his stammering denial. Rather than rescue his Lord, Peter stood frozen with fear while warming his hands at a fire. After his third denial, the rooster crowed, and the rest is history. Peter turned to see Jesus staring at him through the garden trellis. His heart broke, and he ran into the dark night weeping bitterly. Fortunately, this was not the end of the story. The day of Pentecost was only a few months away, and the Lord's use of Peter was far from done. It is his response, though, after his fall, that I want us to consider. Unlike Judas, Peter chose a different path.

First, he did not fight nor deny the fact that he denied Jesus. He allowed his collapse to awaken him to his true condition of helplessness. Peter saw that his strength would never be enough. It is recorded that he wept bitterly. Peter embraced his denial of Jesus for all its ugliness and expressed true remorse. Jesus was not caught off guard by the collapse of Peter's faith. He foretold it would happen. It was the prayer of Jesus that Peter's fall would not be used by Satan to discourage him from future ministry. The devil desires to "sift you as wheat," Jesus said.[202] It is not the fact that men sin but how they respond to it that becomes the most important thing.

Secondly, Peter allowed Jesus to embrace and restore him after the resurrection. One of the resurrection appearances was to Peter alone.[203] The bruised apostle chose a soft landing in the arms of Jesus. Judas, in contrast, chose the thorny shrubbery of regret and hanged himself. For Peter, the prickly bushes of self-pity were rejected for the soft grass of forgiveness and love.

However, to my dismay, Peter rejected the third observation concerning the art of falling. Rather than looking around to see if anyone saw him fall, Peter told the world of his denial. If Mark's gospel is the product of Peter's preaching, as most theologians agree, then it is interesting to note that it is the most descriptive narrative concerning Peter's denial. Rather than hide his sin, Peter told the world what Jesus had done for him. He owned his fall that night, not with the determination to do better, but with a lifelong reliance on God's mercy and strength. Peter stood on the day of Pentecost and delivered a powerful message of redemption. He was fearless and bold as a lion as he stood before the very men who had crucified Jesus Christ. Peter celebrated the grace of Jesus by never trusting himself again. From that day forward, his eyes were on the Savior, not himself. Peter fell to find new heights.

෩෩෩

For the sake of Christ, then, I am content with weaknesses, insults, hardships, persecutions, and calamities. For when I am weak, then I am strong.

2 CORINTHIANS 12:10 ESV

CHAPTER 44

Loneliness

ong before the Lone Ranger kicked up dust with his sidekick Tonto, he trotted about the desert on a mare named Dusty. Not a very exciting name, but I'm sure she was a good horse. Our hero's second stallion was named Silver. Compared to the name Dusty it was a bit of an improvement, and Silver possessed an interesting backstory. She was rescued by the Lone Ranger from an enraged buffalo, and as a result, became his lifelong friend and compadre. The Lone Ranger was the sole survivor of a band of six Texas Rangers. There's something romantic about this lone figure riding into the sunset on his trusty mare, but those who live life in isolation tell a different story.

In 1967, American singer-songwriter Henry Nilsson wrote a song titled, *One*, which included the opening line, "One is the loneliest number that you'll ever do."[204] Nilsson wrote the song after calling a woman and receiving nothing but a busy signal. He stayed on the line, listening to the beep, beep, beep as he wrote the song. It was eventually recorded by the band, Three Dog Night, in 1968. Living with loneliness is a difficult lot, but it is even more challenging when the isolation is the result of living for God. Standing against the current of this age has never been an envious position, and it comes with a cost. Few knew the trail of loneliness more than the Old Testament prophet, Elijah.

By Elijah's word, the heavens had been shut for three years. The crops were drying up, and the cattle were dying. After pronouncing judgement on the sins of King Ahab and the people of Israel, God had removed Elijah to the brook Cherith for his own safety. He was fed there by ravens who brought him bread, possibly stolen from the king's palace. Alone by the brook, he sat watching the land and the people he loved, wither away. It is never popular to speak on God's behalf, especially when the message is not what people want to hear. Preaching the judgment of God will not win you an invitation to speak at a Fourth of July celebration.

After the brook dried up, Elijah was told to go to Zarephath. There he found a widow woman who was gathering sticks to cook her last meal and then die. Elijah made her this promise, "Do not fear; go and do as you have said. But first make me a little cake of it and bring it to me, and afterward make something for yourself and your son. For thus says the LORD, the God of Israel, 'The jar of flour shall not be spent, and the jug of oil shall not be empty, until the day that the LORD sends rain upon the earth.'"[205] She obeyed and reaped the blessing of God. Elijah finally had someone to talk to, and the woman's needs were met in a miraculous way. She even received her son back to life through the prayer of the prophet of God. Even in a drought the Lord always takes care of his own.

After three years, King Ahab was at his wits end. He decided to place a bounty on Elijah's head. However, before the king could find him, the prophet came out of hiding and confronted Ahab. The scene was classic. The king accused Elijah of causing the drought, and the prophet replied that it was he and the people who had turned away from God. Elijah stood his ground against a very powerful man as the true prophets of God have done down through the ages. Centuries later, another man of God stood in isolation to defend the truth concerning the deity of Christ. His name was Athanasius.

Few have demonstrated standing against the world alone like Athanasius of the third century. When Arianism reared its ugly head and sought to lead the church into heresy, Athanasius stood against it. At the council of Nicaea in 325AD, he argued the deity of Christ before the other church leaders and the Roman emperor, Constantine. As Caesars came and went, Athanasius fell in and out of favor. At one point five thousand soldiers surrounded his church in Alexandria, Egypt. They broke down the doors and attempted unsuccessfully to arrest him. On one occasion, the

Roman emperor stated, "Athanasius, the world is against you." He boldly replied, "Well then, Athanasius is against the world."[206]

The loneliness that Elijah experienced was a result of his stand against sin. His goal was never popularity. The prophet's desire was to honor God, and therefore, he was relentless in ministry. Those who walk with God must expect times when the dark shroud of loneliness leaves them discouraged. It happened to Elijah even after his victory on Mount Carmel. However, sometimes the loneliness we experience can slip into something more debilitating.

Anxiety and depression are common to the human experience. Their devastating effects touch all of us in varying degrees at different times of our lives. The fact that we can be surrounded by people we love, and who love us, and yet, experience a deep sense of despair, is one of the great mysteries of life. Depression and anxiety are not simply in our minds. The experience is real and as thorny as a briar patch. It is a swirling, suffocating vacuum that wraps itself around our brain and chokes the joy out of each moment of life. Anxiety brings a tsunami of worry and trepidation crashing in on us. These twin enemies of our soul will not be rooted out by a pill, neither will they be ousted by simply wishing it were not so. The dark clouds arrive at the most unlikely times and for no apparent reason. With a thousand blessings to count and a thousand reasons to be happy, depression and anxiety still creep into our lives. Their crippling effects madden us. Nevertheless, there are real answers that will help during these periods of our lives.

First, understand that depression comes when we abandon the reality of who we are as children of God. We begin to listen to the lies of the enemy. He whispers that we are useless and unworthy when the very opposite is true. God clearly states that we are loved and forgiven; this is our reality. Every life is valuable to God. The Bible declares that we are the very righteousness of Jesus Christ. No performance is necessary to gain his love and grace. He loves us at our worst moment. The only voice that matters is the one that is coming from the throne in Heaven. When the sound of God's voice grows, the voices of circumstances and people shrink. Depression and anxiety are eased when we believe we are unconditionally loved.

Furthermore, depression and anxiety crowd in when we think we are all alone and that no one understands or cares. The mighty prophet Elijah, after his great victory over Baal's false prophets, became terrified of a woman named Jezebel. Running at full sprint from this wicked queen, he ended up in a cave bemoaning his lot in life. Elijah even asked the Lord to take his life. He thought he was the only one who served God. The Lord graciously showed up in the cave and set the record straight. "Yet I will leave seven thousand in Israel, all the knees that have not bowed to Baal, and every mouth that has not kissed him."[207] The army of the Lord is always bigger than we think and closer than we can imagine. He may have them hidden away, but just at the right moment; they will come to the battle.

Finally, tell somebody what you're experiencing, preferably a person you love and trust. Our silence only makes matters worse. The monster seems to grow when we bury it in the shadows. The weight of sadness somehow lifts when we tell someone. There's an old Scottish proverb that goes like this; "A burden shared is lightened but a burden kept is twice the load."

Talking about anxiety and depression gets the creepy thing out of the closet and into the light. The Bible reminds us to carry our burdens to the Lord. "Cast thy burden upon the LORD, and he shall sustain thee: he shall never suffer the righteous to be moved."[208] Tell the Lord what you're feeling and trust that he knows all about the darkness. Remember that the Lord has endured every human temptation that we experience. He's the one person that understands our cares. Anxiety and depression are real, and they hurt, but there are things you can do to combat them that doesn't include popping a pill. One *is* the loneliest number, but you are not alone. Never forget that you and God are always a majority.

Be strong and courageous. Do not fear or be in dread of them, for it is the LORD your God who goes with you. He will not leave you or forsake you.

DEUTERONOMY 31:6 ESV

CHAPTER 45

The Timeless Gospel

P.T. Barnum was once described as the greatest showman on earth. His ability to promote his enterprises and draw crowds was legendary. He understood that people lived ordinary lives, and that they craved the extraordinary, the spectacular. The likes of Tiny Tim, the Bearded Lady, and Jumbo were just a few of Barnum's gifts to the world. The longing to see something amazing is in us all. We happily pay the ticket price to be set back on our heels. We want to see something that entertains us. It is a craving that lives within every human heart. As they say, "There's no business, like show business."

The theater, the movie house, and the circus all have one thing in common. They all satisfy a natural itch within humanity for applause; both in the giving of it, and the receiving. The simple clapping of hands delights both audience and performers alike. However, this desire to impress a crowd under the big top can easily become a stumbling block for the church, and it has done so for the last two thousand years. The words of Oswald Chamber still ring true today, "The abomination "show business" is creeping into the very ranks of the saved and sanctified. "We must get the crowds." We must not; we must keep true to the Cross; His Cross; let folks come and go as they will, let movements come and go, let ourselves be swept along or not, the one main thing is- true to the yoke of Christ His Cross."[209]

Our responsibility within the church is not to provide show-stopping performances each week. We are to stay true to the gospel message and keep it as simple as possible. One of the obsessions of PT Barnum was the ticket sales each night. He demanded to know the count after each show. On the day he died, one of his last questions was not about where he would spend eternity, he asked about the ticket sales. A full tent was his driving motivation. Expanding his income base was Barnum's goal in life. The church must always guard against a mindset that equates a packed auditorium with success. We must also stir clear of business models. Jesus said, "I will build my church..."[210]

Our confidence must be in the gospel of Jesus Christ, not results. The gospel is the power of God leading to the salvation of men. Its message of redemption has not lost any of its efficacy. The Lord is always working in the lives of those around us, whether we see it or not. He takes full responsibility for building his church. We must leave the results in his hands and wait for Heaven to see what he has done through our lives and ministries.

Years ago, I worked for a vending company filling snack machines. One of my stops was a welding shop. It was a rough environment, filled with tough, leathery men. It was not uncommon to have sandwich machines broken into if the correct change was not given or the machine failed to yield its product. I made it my practice to leave gospel tracts at each of my stops including the welding shop. One day, while servicing the machines, a large man approached me. To say he was intimidating would be an understatement. He asked me, in a gruff voice, if I had been leaving the tracts. I mustered up all the strength within me and replied that I had indeed left the pamphlets. I prepared myself to duck. He simply smiled and said that last night he had gotten saved because of reading the tract. I breathed a sigh of relief and congratulated him.

It is always a joy to see the Lord's work in people's lives, but I'm convinced that that experience is the exception, not the rule. It was a thrill to see the fruit of sowing the gospel in that man's life, but more times than not, we are not privy to the moment. Most of the time, we do not see the power of the gospel at work. Why is this so? I believe that the Lord hides most of his work so that we will keep our eyes on him, not his work. One of the first sermons in the early church was met with great opposition and seemed to yield no results.

Stephen was one of the original deacons and the first martyr of the church. Standing faithfully against a devilish crowd of religious Jews, he preached the gospel with unflinching bravery. It was a long and exhaustive sermon, which included a summary of Jewish history with rolling references to the nation's rejections of God. He closed with this stinging rebuke, "You stiff-necked people, uncircumcised in heart and ears, you always resist the Holy Spirit. As your fathers did, so do you."[211] That kind of approach does not sound warm and fuzzy. If you are looking for a *seeker friendly* preacher, Stephen would not be your cup of tea. You don't start a building program with those kinds of sermons. Who could possibly be attracted to Jesus with such a cold and prickly finish to a long and laborious message?

As he closed out his presentation, he looked over the shoulders of his accusers and saw Jesus standing to welcome him to Heaven. He could have kept his vision silent, but he proclaimed it for all to hear. "And he said, "Behold, I see the heavens opened, and the Son of Man standing at the right hand of God."[212] Enraged, Jewish leadership organized a stoning to shut this man up forever. Casting him outside the city they pelted him with rock after rock until he was close to death. Swollen and bloody, he lifted his voice for one last cry. "And falling to his knees he cried out with a loud voice, 'Lord, do not hold this sin against them.' And when he had said this, he fell asleep."[213] At the close of the sermon there was no alter call; no repentant sinners heeded the call to believe. However, there was one man in the crowd who was listening. He was an up-and-coming rabbi.

Stephen could have offered up a silent prayer, but he chose to make his voice heard over the roar of the crowd. Standing there that day was a young rabbi by the name of Saul. This young man was not just a spectator, he was a participant in the stoning. Even more than that, Saul of Tarsus orchestrated the event.

Something happened to Saul that day that changed history. The way Stephen died was unlike anything he had ever seen before, and, as a result, he eventually came to Christ. One of the greatest fish ever caught by the preaching of the gospel was netted by a man who never knew what was on the other end of his hook. Stephen, the first martyr, had dropped his pole, released his net, and walked off the dock into glory. There, flopping on the shoreline, was Paul the apostle and Stephen never knew it. Perhaps, he thought he had failed. His one and only sermon was long and yielded no visible results.

We must leave the results of our ministry with God. Only eternity will reveal what the Lord has done through us. We can only imagine these two men meeting in glory. To say that Stephen was pleasantly surprised when Paul greeted him in Heaven is an understatement.

As we follow Jesus, he makes us to become fishers of men, but the moment we focus on the fishing expedition, we have taken our eyes off Christ. Evangelism is best served when we stop trying to catch men and simply follow the One who fishes for men. The Holy Spirit is the great lover of men's souls, and his work is going on all around us. If we were allowed to see his drawing influence, then our focus would be taken away from the Great Fisherman and onto the fish themselves. Our responsibility is simply to share the message. Setting the hook and pulling in the net is the work of God alone. As C.S. Lewis once wrote, regarding his own salvation, "And so the great Angler played His fish and I never dreamed that the hook was in my tongue."[214]

In the end we will be judged, not by how big a crowd we drew, but by how faithful we were preaching Christ no matter the size of the gathering. The less we care about the ticket sales the better. Any attempt to sensationalize the rugged truth of the gospel or emphasize results over faithfulness is a betrayal of our calling. The attention must be on Christ, not us. Any judgments on success or failure must be left for Heaven's courts. The judgment seat of Christ alone will be the final measure of our ministries. This alone must be the heartbeat of the servant of God. The Lord's work must be truly his work.

⟨⟩

Well done, good and faithful servant. You have been faithful over a little; I will set you over much. Enter into the joy of your master.

MATTHEW 25:23 ESV

CHAPTER 46

Faithful are the Wounds

The book of Proverbs contains short statements drawn from long living. One of the best known and most quoted is a verse about friendship. "Iron sharpens iron, and one man sharpens another."[215] Blade upon blade the dullness is removed but not without discomfort to both knives. There are many who resist the sharpness of another man's counsel because it exposes a difficult and painful blind spot. Wise is the man who allows the words of a friend to penetrate his pride and wound his heart. Courageous is the man who inflicts the wound and then stays to bandage it. It is only when we are wounded that healing can begin. However, there are those who give weak and inadequate counsel. They are what Job called miserable comforters.[216] Nevertheless, it is an interesting observation of human nature that we call to ourselves counselors according to what we *want* to hear, not necessarily what we *need* to hear. Like shopping on the internet, we chose the reviews we want to read.

When shopping for anything, it is wise to read the reviews before making a purchase. We don't always need five stars, but anything less than three and a half is cause for concern. However, reviews do not always give us the clearest picture. There is a human element that should be considered when reading a person's judgement of a product or service, and it has to do with three types of reviewers. First, there is the axe-grinder. This is the disgruntled customer who just wants to hurt the company because of a failed service or faulty product. Usually these are easy to spot because their review quickly dissolves into a personal attack on the company. Secondly, there is the cousin review. You might be able to figure that one out by its title. All favorable marks are given by someone near and dear to a company owned by Cousin Vinnie. Glowing generalities abound to line the pockets of their friend or family. Usually, their last name is withheld. Finally, there is the one you are looking for, the honest review. This analysis is given by someone who is fair and objective. Pros and cons are delivered in an unbiased manner. From this individual, the truth will shine, and a decision can be made. The truth will set you free and help you make a wise purchase. A prudent person will listen to such a reviewer.

Unfortunately, there is a tendency to surround ourselves with those who will agree with everything we say or do. Therefore, we need people in our lives who will tell us the truth. We must have honest folks, who will come alongside us when we have food in our teeth and hand us a mirror. We need friends who will point us in the right direction when we have lost our way. No matter our response, we need people who care enough to confront us when we are wrong because we all have blind spots. If you have someone like that, thank God for them. And by all means don't push them away. We only hurt ourselves when we choose yes-men as our comrades in arms. Nathan the prophet was a force to be reckoned with because he was willing to tell the truth to a very powerful king named David.

The sweet psalmist of Israel had committed adultery with the wife of Uriah. Bathsheba then sent a message to David, months later, telling him that she was pregnant. Instead of facing the consequences of his sin, the king sent her husband to the front of the battle to be killed. With murder, sexual immorality, and an illegitimate child on the way, David acted as if nothing were wrong. After all, he was the King of Israel. No one would dare confront him because he was God's anointed leader. After giving the king time to repent, God sent Nathan to confront his servant. Nathan met David along a rocky path overlooking Jerusalem and told him a story.

"There were two men in one city: the one rich, and the other poor. The rich man had exceeding many flocks and herds: but the poor man had nothing, save one little ewe lamb, which he bought and nourished up: and it grew up together with him, and with his children; it did eat of his own meat, and drink of his own cup, and lay in his bosom, and it was onto him a daughter. And there came a traveler unto the rich man, and he spared to take of his own flock and of his own herd, to dress for the wayfaring man that was come unto him, but he took the poor man's lamb and dressed it for the man that was come to him."[217] Samuel wisely told a story that David could relate to, having been a shepherd from his youth. David was drawn into the emotion of the story having perhaps seen the same injustice done many times. A poor shepherd boy, keeping his humble flock on the hillsides of Israel, might have experienced the extravagant excesses of the rich at the expense of the poor.

As a result, David was outraged and demanded that the rich man be killed. Nathan lowers the boom with no consideration for being gentle. "Behold, you are the man."[218] When you have to say a hard thing, don't sugarcoat it. Say it plainly and with clear eyes because that is what people need to hear. David had spent an entire year living with his sin and would have never faced it without Nathan's rebuke. It takes courage to confront people who can hurt you, but you are not loving them by remaining silent. By refusing to address situations head on, we are simply protecting ourselves. We are revealing our own selfishness and lack of love by turning away from those who need to be rebuked. It is what David Augsburger meant by titling his book, *Caring Enough to Confront*.

Proverbs tells us that, "Faithful are the wounds of a friend."[219] *Faithful* and *friend* are warm and fuzzy words; *wound* is cold and prickly. There is nothing pleasant about a wound. I recently spoke some hard words to a friend who was in a dark place. He recoiled when the blade entered. Defending himself at every turn, he fought back. He commented that these sound like the words of someone who wants to hurt me, not help me. I didn't want to hurt him, but wounds do hurt. I desperately wanted to help him. A doctor takes no pleasure in cutting flesh, but if he doesn't, the infection remains. To my friend my words may have sounded like those of an enemy, but this is the difference. I still stand by him; I still pray for him; I still love him, and at the drop of a hat I would race to his side. Wounds hurt, but the greater hurt is to say or do nothing. The Proverb concludes with, "the kisses of an enemy are deceitful."[220] My friend needed a wound not a kiss.

People don't need axe-grinders or cousin reviews. They need a friend who will wound them and then stay by their side, ready to bind up the wound. I give you fair warning, this process may take years, and you may never see the results in this lifetime. Still go. Make sure there is no beam in your eye and then reach for the speck in your brother's eye. This is homework for the stout-hearted; this is the greatest mark of friendship.

Faithful *are* the wounds of a friend; but
the kisses of an enemy *are* deceitful.

ROVERBS 27:6 KJV

CHAPTER 47

Fearless

In his book, *Facing the Mountain*, Daniel James Brown describes the experience of Japanese Americans after the attack on Pearl Harbor. It was a sad time in our history, as our government violated the constitutional rights of these dear people by placing many of them in internment camps. It is an amazing fact that so many young Japanese men volunteered to fight the Germans in Europe. Brown, in his book, includes many of the exploits of these brave soldiers in Italy as they battled the Nazis. One such conflict occurred in a wooded area called the Vosges, in northern Italy. A group of soldiers from Texas, thereafter, known as the *lost regiment*, had been trapped by the Germans on top of a mountain. Certain death awaited them if they weren't rescued. A regiment of Japanese American soldiers were told to storm the hill and rescue their fellow soldiers. It was a suicide mission, and they all knew it. Facing insurmountable odds, with German tanks firing down on them, Fred Shiosaki and the rest of his company climbed that muddy mountain. Shrapnel flew past them as bullets splintered nearby pine trees. Grabbing onto tree roots, they pulled themselves up toward the enemy. Shiosaki braced for death. But then, something unexpected happened. Fear suddenly vanished, and he was left with an unmistakable sense of calm. Fred Shiosaki experienced a life-changing moment that remained with him his entire life.

"Nothing else mattered. Everything had become extraordinarily sharp- every pebble that flew by, every pine branch that broke overhead, every distant cry, every minute rustling of his mud-caked uniform. He took it all in instantaneously, apprehended it fully, even as he kept firing, reaching for new clips, slamming them into the gun and firing again."[221]

When the fear of death left Shiosaki, a marvelous freedom entered, and life came into clear view. He discovered, to his great surprise, a sense of exhilaration when he counted his own life as expendable for a greater cause. The rescue of the regiment from Texas became his dominating thought as his own life faded from view. During his climb up the mountain, he faced death head on and chose to be fearless. Free from the entanglement of dread, Fred Shiosaki came alive in a way he had never experienced. This truth, and its subsequent experience, has been the birthright of the church since Pentecost. In much the same way that Shiosaki's moment of clarity changed him, the followers of Jesus were changed by the Holy Spirit.

The disciples, who met in the upper room, had been in hiding from the religious authorities in Jerusalem. Jesus told them to stay in the city until the promise of the Holy Spirit had been given. And so, there they remained, in the very town where Jesus had been crucified. When the day of Pentecost came, they stood before a crowd of thousands and boldly preached the gospel. They knowingly risked their lives when they lifted their voices that day. They could have easily been arrested but none of this mattered to them. They lost their fear of death having received life from the Holy Spirit. They now looked at life through the eyes of men who had come alive from the dead, and the fear of death, no longer held them back.

The Bible speaks of a first and a second death. The first death is when we physically die. Our body returns to the dust, and our spirit returns to the God who gave it. The second death occurs when an individual, who has never received Christ, stands before the Great White Throne, and is judged for their sin. They are then cast into the eternal lake of fire, where they will spend eternity. This is the second death. Jesus warned not to fear those who could kill the body but not the soul. Our fear, he said, should be to the One who can destroy both the body and soul in Hell.[222] Jesus conquered death, thus freeing his followers from the fear of God's judgement. Their sin has already been judged on the cross.

In Christ, we are delivered from the fear of the second death. John, in the book of Revelation, was encouraged by the angel, "Blessed and holy is the one who shares in the first resurrection! Over such the second death has no power, but they will be priests of God and of Christ, and they will reign with him for a thousand years."[223] When a believer dies, he receives a new body. Courage in the face of torture and death are possible because we look forward to our eternal home in Heaven where we will walk in our new body.

Faith declares that death is no longer to be feared because it has been swallowed up in life. Let the enemy do his worst and, in the end, we walk down streets of gold. Man cannot touch us unless the hand of God allows it, and if he does, it is for our good and his glory. Even Satan had to ask permission to afflict Job, and even though he suffered, he gained back all he lost two-fold. We are not only to be fearless when faced with death, we are to be fearless in the way we live our lives.

If a preacher allows the deadly poison of fear to seep into his pulpit, he becomes cautious. He chooses non-offensive passages, avoiding abrasive texts. The topic of judgement and Hell are pushed to the back of the shelf in favor of only preaching about Heaven and healing. He eyes the congregation to see if what he is saying is pleasing to their itching ears. The believer who calculates the stranger before him rarely shares the gospel. He wavers to share the message of hope for fear of losing a friend or offending a stranger. Fear is a silent killer that can only be exposed when we begin to ask ourselves some pointed questions. What is the worst that can be done to us? The most pointed question of all, may be the most important. What is the source of our fear?

Joseph of Arimathea was a member of the Sanhedrin. He was wealthy, powerful and a secret disciple of Jesus. We are not left to our imagination regarding his motive for remaining in the shadows. He hid his faith in Christ because he was afraid of the Jews. He allowed men to silence him. However, something changed after the crucifixion that redefined him for proceeding generations. There was something in the death of Jesus that caused Joseph to abandon his fear and boldly ask for the body of Jesus from the most powerful political figure in the land, Pilate.

As he stood watching the cross from a distance, he no doubt heard the cry of Jesus, "It is finished."[224] Joseph witnessed the worst that man can do, and yet, in Jesus he heard the shout of victory. He understood, in that life-changing moment, that there was something greater than his own life. There was a cause greater than his own life; it was the glory of God. Joseph embraced the One who conquered death, and in so doing, released his grip on life. Along with losing his life, he lost the crippling effect of fear. He went with Nicodemus, and together, they took down the body of Jesus from the cross. Covered with blood he had never been so free. Carrying the dead body of Jesus was a light thing compared to the fear he had carried all his life.

It is the preservation of our own lives that is the source of our fear. Once we embrace death as the doorway into life, fear flies away like a flock of frightened geese. When Ignatius, one of the early church martyrs, was facing the flames, he replied, "I esteem no visible things, nor yet invisible things, so that I may get or obtain Christ Jesus. Let the fire, the gallows, the wild beasts, the breaking of bones, the pulling asunder of members, the bruising of my whole body, and the torments of the devil in hell itself come upon me, so that I may win Christ Jesus."[225] When faced with the attack of Satan, the saints in Revelation were described in this way, "And they have conquered him by the blood of the Lamb and by the word of their testimony, for they loved not their lives even unto death."[226] It is the dying leaf that displays the most beautiful color. Joseph of Arimathea finally understood that truth, and as a result, no longer feared what man could do to him.

Jesus said that unless a grain of wheat falls into the ground and dies it abides alone, but once that seed dies, it yields much fruit. Our lives only begin when we charge up the mountain of fear with the reckless abandonment of faith. The exhilaration that Fred Shiosaki sensed, as he stormed the enemy, is to be the living reality of the Christian every day of his life. Fred counted his life worthy of the sacrifice that he would have to make to rescue those men. Jesus Christ is worthy of our lives, and if need be, the sacrifice of our death. As Paul reminded us, "For me to live is Christ and to die is gain."[227]

When it was evening, there came a
rich man of Arimathea, named Joseph,
who also was a disciple of Jesus.

MATTHEW 27:57 ESV

CHAPTER 48

True Salvation

I love my crockpot. The other morning, I filled it with a roast, carrots, potatoes, an onion, and a couple cans of cream of mushroom soup. After setting it on low, I went to work. Halfway through the morning I broke out in a cold sweat. Did I plug it in? Oh, the ravages of old age, the cruelty of a dissipating mind. Terror crept across my soul with the thought of my roast spoiling in the pot. I reassured myself that if I made it home by early afternoon, I would have time to set it on high and have a shot at dinner by seven. I arrived home and cracked the door. I was instantly greeted with the glorious odor of a roast simmering in its own juices. I closed the door, breathed a sigh of relief, and went to water my plants.

When something is cooking, you always smell it. For good or for bad, you smell it. When a life has been transformed by the Son of God, there is always the evidence of a good odor. That which is overflowing from the heart cannot be hid. Life will always provide proof for its existence by outward expression. A baby cries, eats, and well, you know the rest. The branch that bends without breaking and bares the bud of springtime possesses the life of the root. When a spring of water finds its way onto dry ground, the earth produces fruit. Jesus said a good tree will bear good fruit, and an evil tree will bear evil fruit. He also said, "I am the vine; you are the branches. Whoever abides in me and I in him, he it is that bears much fruit, for apart from me you can do nothing."[228]

Once an individual places faith in Christ, they receive the gift of the Holy Spirit. All that Jesus accomplished in redemption is applied to an individual through the person of the Holy Spirit. The full concentration of a follower of Christ must remain on the work of Jesus within and a growing knowledge of the Word of God. Life change is an organic process. It is a natural outcome of God's work within the human heart. Wherever Christ is present, there is transformation.

However, we all have doubts from time to time whether we truly know the Lord, and the Bible does not leave us without reassurance. The Scriptures give us certain benchmarks to help us know that we are on the right path. Being confident of our salvation is vital. If we are constantly questioning our faith, the results will be insecurity and fear. James tells us that the one who doubts is like the waves of the sea driven by the wind.[229] In contrast, Jesus said the truth will set us free. It is the desire of God that our fellowship with him, and walk in this world, is stable and strong. We need to hang our hat on the concrete hook of Scripture, not on an emotional experience or feeling. Saving faith brings change, and that change has specific characteristics.

The purpose of John's letter to the churches of Asia Minor was to reassure believers that they possessed eternal life. The apostle was not writing to those outside the church but to those who were saved and who needed confidence to press on to the kingdom. The book of First John was a litmus test for those who were struggling with their assurance. He wanted them to be grounded in truth so that their joy would be complete.

John declared God is light and in him there is no darkness. He does not ask the believer about his lifestyle; he states that he dwells in light. The mind of a true believer has been adjusted to recognize light verses darkness and to respond accordingly. A believer confesses sin and rejoices in forgiveness. John emphasized the joy of fellowship with the Father and with one another. Our love for the brethren is also evidenced by our faithfulness to be a part of his church. Our relationship with the world system has also been altered. Even though we live in this world, we are no longer a part of it. These are the high-water marks by which we know that we have eternal life.

All living creatures operate based on their DNA. All living beings, great and small, live out their lives according to the passions and drives within. Lions roar and chickens scratch in the dirt, not because they are taught to do so, but because it is in their nature. Do you love the light of

God's presence rather than the darkness of sin? When you sin, is confession your immediate response? A true believer will want to spend time with God's people. Is your love directed toward the Father or the world? The man who truly knows Christ will keep his commandments, not because it is his duty, but out of the joy he finds his heart. It is the life of Jesus within that motivates the believer toward holy living. These are the true tests that shed light on whether a man or woman knows the Lord. A true believer will stumble at times, but in the end, he will stand.

James, the half-brother of Jesus, said it clearly and without apology. "Faith without works is dead," and then he asked the question, "Can a faith which produces no works save you?"[230] It is a rhetorical question with an obvious answer. No! There is a type of faith which is nothing more than intellectual assent to certain truths. It is not saving faith. A dead faith may bind a man to be in church every Sunday out of duty, but it cannot stir his soul to worship. The kind of faith that saves a man is a repentant, moral decision to receive Christ. This kind of decision alters a man down to his very core, changing both his direction and his internal desires.

My good friend, Mike walked into a bar after his conversion and instantly knew he was in the wrong place. No brother was there to turn him around and send him back home; he however, walked out of that bar never to return. Mike's heart had been changed, and as a result, his desires were dramatically altered.

The question is not whether you go to church or read your Bible. It is not about singing in the choir or preaching in a pulpit. It is whether there is a desire within you to be among God's people, to study the Scriptures, and to serve the Lord. The marks of true salvation are indisputably clear. The proof is in the pudding and the pudding is action. A man or woman who has trusted Christ is truly a new creature and it shows.

What good is it, my brothers, if someone says
he has faith but does not have works?

JAMES 2:14 ESV

CHAPTER 49

Roots

Charles Dickens was a brilliant writer who excelled at producing several rags to riches narratives with unforgettable characters. Oliver Twist, Tiny Tim, and Pip in *Great Expectations* were just a few of the characters Dickens used to paint his stories with a sympathetic brush regarding London's most disadvantaged. A story about a pauper who is really a prince draws us in like a moth to a light. Books line shelves telling tales of those who grew up in humble situations only to find out that their true father was the king or some wealthy landowner. We all long for a pot of gold at the end of a rainbow. We love reading those stories because we all cheer for the underdog. Perhaps, the attraction lies in the fact that we want to discover noble bloodlines in our family, or, better yet, a lost inheritance waiting to be claimed. Whatever the case, digging around in our roots can lead to amazing and sometimes disturbing revelations.

Recently, I have been reading my grandmother's genealogy. It was given to me years ago, and it chronicles the story of the Saxton clan in upstate New York. It begins with George Saxton, who, in the 1600s chose the wrong side of the Cromwell Rebellion and was forced to flee England. It ends, for me at least, with the birth of my grandmother in 1889. It is an amazing story of a family who forged their way in a new country, finally settling in a wilderness town at the foot of Oswego Lake. In the last few pages, my name appears, but only as a footnote. Alas, a footnote.

Most entries are simple. He was born and then he died. She married, gave birth to these children and then she died. The reward of such a study, though, are the snippets along the way that are a bit longer and more in depth. Such as, *Delia Saxton Palmer left her husband Frederick, walking home from Elks Creek the morning after her wedding night.* It would have been interesting to know the details of that story. Delia was no doubt disappointed in some way. We can only imagine. Or, *a limb fell on John Saxton on April 1st, 1821, calling him away to mingle with his native clay.* Hopefully his wife wasn't holding the axe.

However, the one that caught my attention was an entry concerning my, great, great grandfather, James W. Saxton. He was the second son born to Simeon and Amelia Saxton in 1835, but he was not the first to be named James W. His younger brother died six months before his birth and bore the same name. To name a second son with the exact same name of a child who had died is an odd thing indeed. What would cause a mother to do this? Was there something in the death of her first-born son that disturbed her? Perhaps, she was to blame somehow. We can only speculate. If the fascinating parts of stories are in the details, we are many times left wanting to know more. To study genealogies effectively requires a keen eye and the ability to connect the dots. Wild speculation aside, students of their family's ancestry must learn to read between the lines. The joy in discovery is realized when one sees their connection to the past through their family roots.

Now whether you go in for such things as genealogies, the truth is, we are all connected to a flow of life from long ago. There is no escaping the fact that we all descended from a group of people that we resemble. We all inherited traits from people we have never met from lands far away. Their stories, filled with life-changing decisions and character-building moments, are in some mysterious way, a part of us. This was true of Jesus Christ in a unique way.

It is interesting to note that Matthew and Luke are the only gospels which include a genealogy. Matthew's account tracks the heritage of Jesus back to Abraham. David is also mentioned early in the list even though he was born later. Apparently, Jessie's youngest son factors largely in the story Matthew writes. The mention of these two men, Abraham, and David, establish the Jewish roots of Jesus and his right to claim the kingship of Israel. Matthew's account also mentions four women, which is quite unusual for Jewish genealogies. Genealogies deal with fathers, not mothers; regardless, these four women are included on the list: Tamar, Rahab, Ruth, and Bathsheba. The last name on the list, Bathsheba, shows up as the *wife of Uriah*. Obviously, God still considered Bathsheba to be Uriah's wife, not David's.

A careful examination of these four women reveal that the family line of Jesus had a questionable past. Tamar tricked her father-in-law into having sex with her because he had denied her the right to his youngest son in marriage. Rahab was a prostitute who lived in Jericho. Ruth was a Moabitess, and her nationality would have been very offensive to the Jews. Bathsheba committed adultery with King David and then stood by as David sent her husband to the front of the battle to be killed. All this history could have been swept under the rug if Matthew would have just excluded their names from the genealogy. After all, if his desire was to present Jesus as the King of Israel, you would think an ugly past would be hidden away. God obviously wanted to teach us a very important truth.

Jesus was sinless in word and deed, and yet, he identified with sinful man. His connection to humanity was not academic in nature. The Son of God was fully man, and his humanity was given to him by his mother. He possessed a human nature, just as we do, but without the taint of sin. He was man as if he were not God and God as if he were not man. He was the God-Man. His connection to us is best exemplified in the names listed in his genealogy, and those four women reflect his union with those who had a checkered past. There is great importance in this fact.

Our genealogy tracks back farther than we can trace on any internet site. The Bible declares that our roots go back to the first Adam, and, as a result, we were all born in a condition called sin. The reality of our sin nature is an undeniable reality. We did not choose Adam's family line; it was chosen for us by the head of humanity. As the old saying goes, *we are not sinners because we sin, we sin because we are sinners.* Sin is the condition we find ourselves in when we accept God's estimate of things. Try as we might, we cannot break free from Adam's line apart from a new birth. We did not choose our origin, but we can decide our destiny. Since we were born into Adams' family, we must be born again to enter a new family.

Watchman Nee writes this, "But in order to bring us into his new kingdom God must do something new in us. He must make us new creatures. Unless we are created anew we can never fit into the new realm. However educated, however cultured, however improved it be, flesh is still flesh. Our fitness for the new kingdom is determined by the creation to which we belong. Our ultimate suitability for the new realm hinges on the question of origin. That which is of the old creation can never pass over into the new."[231]

Through the sacrifice of Christ on the cross, we can be free from the old creation and our heredity of sin. When we recognize Jesus died for us and believe in him, we instantly gain a brand-new genealogy. Our roots no longer go back to Adam. Our heritage is now found in Jesus Christ and his perfect righteousness. Have you claimed his heritage as your own today? Believe on Christ, and you are welcomed into a new, eternal family.

This poem was included at the end of the Saxton genealogy; "If you could see your ancestors, all standing in a row, there might be some of them perhaps you wouldn't care to know. But here's another question which requires a different view, if you could meet your ancestors, would they be proud of you!" Our lives are a part of the cycle of life with all those who have gone before us influencing us and those who will come after us whom we will impact. No man is an island. Receiving Christ dramatically alters our genealogy and gives us a new identity. Our new identity has the potential to affect generations to come.

⊙⟶⟶⟵○

A generation goes, and a generation comes, but the earth remains forever.

ECCLESIASTES 1:4 ESV

CHAPTER 50

The Classroom

"All the world is a stage." If that old saying was true back when it was first uttered, it certainly rings true today. Phones and tablets are everywhere recording us when we least expect it. The internet is readily available to send our latest awkward performance around the world with the click of a mouse. When the video is posted, we anxiously wait to see if we will be booed or applauded. Being on our best behavior has never been more important. Also, the past is no longer the past. We are now held libel for what we did and said in junior high, which makes me grateful they didn't have surveillance cameras when I was growing up. Big brother in the classroom would have been enough to lock me up in the slammer for twenty to life. My science teacher, Mr. Appel, could have sent me away to pound rocks for a good long time.

To the followers of Jesus, the world is not only a stage; it is a classroom. Every circumstance we face and every person we meet is an opportunity to learn something new and grow in grace. The Master designs each day with a different lesson plan in mind and some days end with a pop quiz. At the end of the school year, when all schoolwork is past and summer vacation lies ahead, the Lord sometimes surprises us with a final exam. Abraham, along with his wife, Sarah, faced such a test toward the end of their pilgrimage. It involved someone who was precious to them both.

Abraham's relationship with God had had its ups and downs, its ebb and flow. His dealings with his nephew Lot, as he rescued him out of Sodom, revealed a man who deeply trusted God. On another, less faith-filled day, he was faced with the possibility of being killed by a wicked king. Scared for his life, Abraham lied about Sarah being his wife. For this man of God, there were days he was called to the front of the class and commended, and there were days he was sent to the corner to think about his behavior. However, God never gave up on his servant. This elderly couple had waited all their lives to have a child, and when Isaac was born their world came alive. As they worked to raise him in their old age, he soon became the apple of their eye. The entire focus of their lives had been placed on Isaac, and that is always a path that leads to a hollow existence. The Bible states that God is jealous over his children.[232] We view jealousy in a negative light, but with God that is not true. For his own glory, and our good, God is always to be the central focus of our lives. When others take that place, we are drinking water from a stagnant and poisonous well. To bring the founder of the Jewish nation back from the brink of idol worship, Abraham was called to take his only son up the side of a mountain and offer him as a sacrifice.

There is no mention of Abraham telling Sarah what he was about to do. He simply packed what he needed on the back of a donkey and left early in the morning. This test was between God and Abraham. Why would God, who condemned the Canaanites for sacrificing their sons and daughters in the fire, tell Abraham to kill his own son? God was doing something more than just testing his servant, he was deepening him.

Truth that has entered our minds does not become a living reality until it is mixed with faith. Life's experiences offer that opportunity. "Faith is not rational; therefore, it cannot be worked out on the basis of logical reason; it can only be worked out on the implicit line of living obedience."[233] A man might be properly instructed on how to use an umbrella, but the test of his knowledge comes during a rainstorm.

A man may say he believes a certain thing, but he does not know this is true until the storm comes, and then the pencils are sharpened for the final exam. It is easy to say we believe in Heaven, but when a loved one goes there, is our heart truly comforted? When good health is removed, and we face the possibility of a debilitating disease, do we believe in the goodness of God? When the test comes, do we stand strong in faith, or do our knees buckle at what we perceive to be a cruel reality? Trials do not build our faith; they reveal what we truly believe and then offer us an opportunity to reach out to God in a new and deeper way. They sometimes expose what needs to be removed from our lives for us to grow in faith. Nevertheless, it is only human to ask why the offering of Abraham's only son as a sacrifice. After all, he was the son that had been promised.

Abraham's walk to the mountain included silent hours of reflection. He did not discuss with Isaac what he was about to do, neither did he mention it to his servant. This final test was conducted in a classroom where only the teacher and student were present. When God is testing us, it is best to remain silent and listen. Jesus said that when we pray, we should go into a closet. When we are fasting, we should not let anyone know it. Our walk with God is a very intimate and personal matter. As Abraham raised the knife to kill his son, his heart no doubt trembled.

This man of God had been told years earlier that his descendants would be as the stars of heaven. Here was the lad Isaac, now a teenager, and he was being told to sacrifice him as a burnt offering. Abraham was being told to do something that directly contradicted an earlier promise of God. The Lord had a purpose for what he had asked Abraham to do on Mt. Moriah. He uses what he orchestrates in life to bring us to an end of ourselves. This is what Abraham had to learn; when we are trusting anything or anyone else, we are not trusting God. Abraham's hope was in Isaac not in the God of Isaac and that needed to change. His eyes were focused on the promise rather than the Promise Giver. The people and things that we hold tightly belong to God, and at times, must be released. Otherwise, they become a stumbling block in our relationship with the Lord. Corrie Ten Boom, a survivor of the Holocaust, lost everything. However, the one thing the Nazis could not take away was her faith in Jesus Christ.

In his willingness to give his son to God in death, Abraham gained Isaac back in a greater way. Jesus taught that the love we have for God must outstrip all human relationships. When this occurs, the love that we have for others becomes possible in a way we have never known before. Our love for those God has given us grows exponentially when the Lord is our singular focus. To bring us to that place, he is willing to use extreme measures.

It is the tendency of human beings to become obsessive over what they set their hearts upon. It is the way God has created us. In this great classroom of life there is never a recess, or a bell rung to signal the end of day. Day and night our Heavenly Father watches over us to bring us to a place of divine passion. He does not rest until we find our complete rest in him. Jesus must be our great obsession because anything or anyone else is unworthy of our consideration. Until he is the satisfaction of our hearts and the joy in our souls, he will continue to instruct us in the night watches. So, let's all sit up in our chairs, sharpen our pencils and listen to our Teacher. We will be tested on the material.

<hr />

When Abram was ninety-nine years old the LORD appeared to Abram and said to him, I am God Almighty; walk before me, and be blameless.

GENESIS 17:1 ESV

CHAPTER 51

The Miracle of Redemption

T he salvation of the soul of man is a divine intervention with eternal implications. It is the greatest of all miracles. However, God can do nothing with the soul that attempts to establish his or her own righteousness. He, thus, has no desire that men try to be good or moral. Until mankind gives up all hope of saving himself, God stands in the shadows and waits. The unbeliever can do nothing to please God.[234] Simply helping man along the path of life would be like giving a blind man a roadmap or a deaf man a piece of music to enjoy. His hope is that men will see themselves as utterly hopeless. "Jesus answered him, 'Truly, truly, I say to you, unless one is born again, he cannot see the kingdom of God.'"[235]

Likewise, God can do nothing for the man who makes the excuse that it is difficult to be saved. It is easy to be born again because the Lord Jesus has done all the work. Our empathy must never be with the sinner. Our sympathy must be with God, who spared not his own Son to make the sinner holy. To offer reasons for refusing God's offer of salvation reveals a deep seeded pride and a rebellious spirit. It carries with it the attitude of, *I am a special case. God must work a little harder to save a man like me.*

It takes the work of the Holy Spirit to reveal our depravity. Apart from the awakening Spirit of God, we would all be hopelessly lost, marching blindly toward the abyss of eternity without God. These truths must be revealed to us as the Lord opens our hearts. And yet, the moment we cry out in desperation, he rushes to us like a mighty wind. Being born from above means that life has been placed within us from Heaven itself. There is nothing inside of a man that God can use to reach him. There is no spark within the heart of man that God can fan into a flame. Mankind is spiritually dead and must be awakened by the Spirit of God. All the work must be outside of a man entering him at the moment he is redeemed. Man can do nothing other than decide to believe. He must choose to be saved.

The simplicity of the gospel, combined with the fact that we cannot discover it apart from his revealing Spirit, compels our gratitude. The path that leads to the cross and forgiveness is a trail that the Lord must blaze for us. Faith does not save a man; it is Christ who redeems. God uses our faith as a conduit, but the saving is God's work alone. Faith is like a straw we place in a milkshake. The straw is simply used as a channel to receive the shake. This was true in the life of a man named Philip, who was one of the early deacons in the church at Jerusalem.

As Philip was preaching in the town of Samaria the Lord blessed mightily. A revival had broken out and the town was electric with joy. Suddenly, the Spirit caught Philip up, and he found himself in a desert all alone. Standing there, scratching his head, he saw a chariot approaching. The Lord told him to join the chariot, and so, he ran to catch up with it. When the door of the chariot opened, he was introduced to an Ethiopian eunuch who was traveling back to his country, having gone to Jerusalem to worship. The eunuch was studying the book of Isaiah. Philip asked him if he understood what he read, and his response revealed a man who was seeking truth. He replied, "How can I understand except some man guide me?"[236] The eunuch was reaching out to Philip for answers.

Philip climbed up into the chariot and beginning at the very spot that the man was reading led him to the Lord. It was a God-appointed moment for the Ethiopian eunuch. The seeking heart met the revealing Spirit of God, and the result was the man's salvation. The eunuch was baptized and then continued his journey back to his homeland. The country of Ethiopia would now hear the gospel from one of the most powerful men in the land.

Behold, his mercy to all of us. We were blind and sitting alone in a dark room all alone. We had no idea where we were or how to escape our dilemma. A hand reached out to ours, guided us to door, and opened our eyes. He gave us the ability to understand the gospel, and we cried out to Jesus. We can claim no merit for knowing the truth. Everything we know has been revealed to us by God's Spirit. Gratitude is more than an attitude; it is a realization that all we possess in life is a gift from God.

Jesus told his followers that the prophets of the Old Testament longed to see what they were experiencing in his ministry on earth. Mighty men like Moses and Abraham did not possess what the humblest believer has today in Christ. We know the blessed Holy Spirit in an abiding way, along with the sweetness of Christ within our hearts. The knowledge of these things is beyond comprehension. Let us never forget that we were once in darkness, and it was God who opened our eyes. In these dark days, the true light of the gospel still shines, and God desires for all men to be saved.

Recently, I had a conversation with an elderly lady concerning her need for Christ. She believed her good works would be enough to take her to Heaven. Having been taught this as a young girl in her church, she refused to be convinced otherwise. Together, we read the Bible, which states, it is by grace we are saved, not by our good works.[237] Regardless, she held firm. Side by side, we compared what she had been taught and what God's word clearly teaches concerning her need to be saved. I'd like to tell you she sided with God, but she did not. She embraced the lies men had told her rather than the God who never lies. She rejected God's word, choosing instead to remain in the darkness of her sin.

The need to be taught the truth at a young age is so important. Paul reminded his protégé Timothy that from a young child he had known the Scripture. When the truth is planted in a child, it has eternal effect, but the opposite is also true. When a lie is told by respected men or women, in a religious setting, it has a powerful impact on a young heart. That dear elderly lady held onto falsehood in the light of truth from the Bible. The battle is real, and the stakes are eternal.

When the rich man lifted his eyes in Hell, and realized it was too late, he asked that Lazarus be sent to his five brothers to warn them not to come to this *place of torment*.[238] Abraham responded that they have Moses and the prophets to warn them. The rich man argued that if one came back from the dead then they would listen. Abraham countered by saying that if they will not believe the Scripture neither will they believe, even if one came back from the grave. Jesus *did* come back from the dead, and the same Pharisees who refused to believe the prophecies regarding the Messiah, rejected the resurrection miracle. To believe in the gospel is a moral choice, not an intellectual decision. Those who reject the gospel are willfully turning away from the truth.

My elderly friend and I concluded with a prayer. I asked the Lord to open her heart and that was the end of our time together. Tempted to be discouraged, I decided instead to trust in the power of the Lord to open her eyes. I was reminded anew that it takes the Lord to bring us to the place that we believe we are sinners and that we need a Savior.

A few months later, I sat with a different lady and shared the gospel. She had also been raised in a church where good works were the means of salvation. She had been taught that the way to Heaven was through her efforts to be a good person. As I shared the verses that spoke of her being a sinner, her heart became heavy. When asked if she would like to receive Christ, she replied, "Oh yes!" After we prayed together, tears filled her eyes as joy flooded her soul. She immediately began to tell everyone she met that she had been saved. The miracle of salvation is a wonder to behold. If the Lord has opened your heart, never forget that it was by his grace it happened. The miracle of redemption is the Lord's work.

෮෩෮

For by grace are ye saved through faith, and that not of yourselves; it is the gift of God. Not of works, lest any man should boast.

EPHESIANS 2:8,9 KJV

CHAPTER 52

The Pathos of God

J esus wept. It is the shortest verse in the Bible and perhaps one of the most revealing. It occurred when Jesus was among a crowd of people who were mourning the death of a man named Lazarus. Overcome by emotion, Jesus joined their grief and suddenly burst into tears. He experienced what the Greeks called, *pathos.* Pathos is a word from which we get our word passion. His reaction confirms the Old Testament prophecy that he would be a man of sorrow and acquainted with grief. [239] However, it also reveals a truth that is difficult for us to understand. The God who created all things and reigns over his created order has emotions. He feels deeply about his creation and cares for mankind more than we can comprehend. The Lord Almighty, who is high and lifted up, holy and distinct from all created beings, eternal in the heavens, feels the same range of emotions as mankind. God experiences anger, sorrow, joy, and a myriad of feelings. God is an emotional being. This is a hard truth to comprehend much less explain.

In much the same way, man's reaction to his own emotional life has been varied. The ancient Greeks separated their schools of thought into two categories: Epicureanism and Stoicism. The former emphasized the idea of *eat, drink, and be merry,* while the latter chose to refrain from any enjoyment or passion in life. Both extremes are to be rejected, and yet, Christianity, through the ages, has adopted the mentality of the Stoic. In response to the pagan world, where immorality rules the day, the church has reacted with extreme legalism and teachings that attempt to restrain the passions of life by edict. The seers and monks who inhabited monasteries throughout the Middle Ages give testament to this Stoic methodology.

In contrast to this hollow approach to Christianity is a God who celebrates his children. Zephaniah suggests that God dances over us. "The LORD your God is in your midst, a mighty one who will save; he will rejoice over you with gladness; he will quiet you by his love; he will exult over you with loud singing."[240] The term, *exult over you* in the Hebrew means to spin around with violence, literally to dance. He has placed this same passion within us, to dance before him as David once did. Our lives are burning torches, lit brightly by the love of God. The Lord's love for us defines our worth, igniting us with *pathos*. The source of God's dance is his intense love for us.

AW Tozer wrote this concerning the love of God, "From God's other known attributes we may learn much about His love. We can know, for instance, that because God is self-existent, His love had no beginning; because He is eternal, His love can have no end; because He is infinite, it has no limit; because He is holy, it is the quintessence of all spotless purity; because He is immense, His love is an incomprehensibly vast, bottomless, shoreless sea before which we kneel in joyful silence and from which the loftiest eloquence retreats confused and abashed."[241] Like endless waves crashing on the shoreline, the love of God relentlessly washes over our souls until we can no longer deny its fervor and passion. In that moment, that which we can no longer define, has become our most defining feature.

In the song, *The Love of God*, Frederick M Lehman writes this, "The love of God is greater far than tongue or pen can ever tell; it goes beyond the highest star and reaches to the lowest hell; the guilty pair bow down with care, God gave his son to win; his erring child He reconciled, and pardon from his sin." He concludes, "Could we with ink the ocean fill, and were the skies of parchment made, were every stalk on earth a quill, and every man a scribe by trade; to write the love of God above would drain the ocean dry; nor could the scroll contain the whole, though stretched from sky to sky."[242] Lehman beautifully captured, with rhyme and meter, the inexhaustible love of God. His words were appropriately extravagant, and they have moved the hearts of many throughout the years.

For some, though, the thought that God has emotions, such as love, is a difficult concept to digest. This is partly true because of the quagmire of our own emotions. Among the three elements that reflect the image of God in man, will, intellect, and emotion, it is the latter that we fear the most. This is because feelings are many times impossible to control. They explode on the scene invoking reactions beyond our ability to corral. We are at our worst when suddenly overcome with emotion. We all tend to say and do things we regret after we have *cooled down*. Moses became so angry at his fellow Jews that he struck a rock instead of speaking to it, and it cost him dearly. We use the term, "I lost my temper," indicating that we must keep it caged somehow. Decisions made during emotional times in our lives usually don't pan out to our good. Perhaps, that is why we have all been told not to *trust our feelings*.

However, God has created us as emotional beings, meant to express passion and feeling. To deny this element of our make-up is to limit our humanity and stunt the work of God in our lives. The fact that Jesus wept at the tomb of Lazarus, speaks to us of the importance of grieving when we lose a loved one. The Lord struggled with intense emotions in the Garden of Gethsemane. He did not hold back expressing the agony he felt due to the death he would have to soon endure. There are agonizing moments in our lives when our hearts are crushed. At these times, it is right and fitting to pour out our hearts to God. David, writing in the Psalms, cried out to the Lord expressing anger, fear, and at times, voicing his complaints against his Creator. We were meant to express emotions, especially when they are negative in nature.

Not only did the Lord feel grief at the tomb of Lazarus, but he also displayed the righteous anger of God while walking in the temple one day. When he turned tables over and drove out the moneychangers, he was full of fury. Those greedy men, who took advantage of the pilgrims who had come to Jerusalem to worship, were making a mockery of a sacred place. Worshiping God was meant to be an expression of love and devotion, but the moneychangers were profiting at their expense. Church leaders, who use the church to steal, lie, and oppress true followers of God, deserve the wrath of the congregants which they falsely serve. It is a form of righteous indignation to become red-faced as revelations of scandals emerge within the church. When sexual sins arise, it is wrong and harmful to suppress the anger we feel.

Likewise, Jesus was angry at the hypocrisy of the Scribes and Pharisees. They condemned others while violating their own commandments, and Jesus was justified in his wrath. "But woe to you, scribes and Pharisees, hypocrites! For you shut the kingdom of Heaven in people's faces. For you neither enter yourselves nor allow those who would enter to go in."[243] Solomon, when he wrote the book of Ecclesiastes, clearly stated that there was a time to refrain from embracing.

It is a well-known fact that Jesus felt compassion to all who came to him. His ability to feel the pain of others was immense beyond our understanding. Jesus was born without sin, and therefore, Adam's sin nature had no effect on him. G. Campbell Morgan suggested that one of the results of sin was, in part, to deaden our emotions. It is possible that what we experience on the scale of our emotions is only a small degree in relation to what Jesus felt. If this is true, we can understand that what he experienced in life was intense on every level.

Subsequently, when he looked out over the crowd that had come to hear him preach, he saw them as sheep without a shepherd. When the Samaritan woman came to draw water from a well, Jesus spoke to her with kindness even though she was an outcast. The woman who had an issue of blood, who simply wanted to touch the hem of his garment, was made whole by his compassionate touch. It is not a far stretch to believe that he has this same compassion for us. Sinners always find a friend in Jesus.

However, the greatest display of the *pathos* of God was seen when Jesus shouted, "It is finished."[244] It was the cry of a victorious king, who had just conquered in battle. The roar of the Lion of Judah occurred moments before he returned to his Father. When Jesus banished sin, his emotions exploded with grandeur unknown to human experience.

Oswald Chambers said this, "The teaching of the New Testament presents the passion of life. Stoicism has come so much into the idea of the Christian life that we imagined a stoic is the best type of Christian; but just where Stoicism seems most like Christianity, it is most adverse. The stoic overcomes the world by passionlessness, by eviscerating all personal interest out of life until he is a mere submissive recording machine. Christianity overcomes the world by passion, not passionlessness."[245] *Faith is the victory,* wrote Paul, and since that is true, then it is our faith and belief in the passion of God which lights us on fire. We walk confidently into the battle with our hands held high proclaiming the passion of God for the world.

Since his love triumphs over our failures, his joy should be *our* joy. Since he dances over his children, his chosen ones, should we not today dance for joy. Passion for life and living is a gift from God.

ᏬᎷᎶ

On the last day of the feast, the great day,
Jesus stood up and cried out, If anyone thirsts,
let him come to me and drink.

JOHN 7:37 ESV

Other Books by M.J. Gaylor

The Well

The Seventh Trail: Journey to the Well Of Chayah

Man's Search for Cabadgery

bisbeesworld.org

End Notes

1   Luke 2:52 ESV
2   1 Corinthians 13:11 ESV
3   Ibid.
4   1 Corinthians 3:1 ESV
5   Galatians 4:19 ESV
6   Romans 1:11 ESV
7   2 Corinthians 5:16,17 ESV
8   Luke 24:11 ESV
9   John 3:13 ESV
10 Psalm 39:6 ESV
11 Judges 14:2 ESV
12 Judges 14:3 ESV
13 John 15:5 ESV
14 Ecclesiastes 1:2 ESV
15 www.brainyquote.com › quotes › honus_wagner_140023
16 Colossians 1:27 ESV
17 Galatians 4:20 ESV
18 John 15:4 ESV
19 2 Peter 1:3 ESV
20 augustinianspirituality.org › augustinequotes
21 1 Corinthians 6:7 ESV
22 Luke 23:43 ESV
23 Isaiah 61:3 ESV
24 https://www.goodreads.com/quotes/578644-love-is-friendship-that-has-caught-fire-it-is-quiet
25 Chesterton, G.K. *Orthodoxy* (Snowball Classic Publishing), 1098.
26 1 John 3:2 ESV
27 Luke 7:41,42 ESV

28 Luke 7:43 ESV

29 Luke 7:44 ESV

30 John 3:16 ESV

31 https://www.urbandictionary.com › define.php?term=coddiwomple

32 Hebrews 11:8 ESV

33 Covey, Stephen, *The Seven Habits of Highly Effective People* (Simon & Schuster), 2020.

34 Chambers, Oswald, *The Complete Works of Oswald Chambers* (Discovery House), 687.

35 John 14:12

36 John 6:20 ESV

37 Matthew14:28,29 ESV

38 Matthew 14:30 ESV

39 Numbers 20:10-13 ESV

40 Deuteronomy 33 ESV

41 Deuteronomy 4:35-37 ESV

42 Lewis, C.S., *The Beloved Works of C.S. Lewis, Surprised by Joy* (Inspirational Press), 125.

43 1 Kings 11:3 ESV

44 Song of Solomon 8:6 ESV

45 1Corinthians 13:4-8 ESV

46 www.gutenburg.org/ebboks/4507

47 Ibid.

48 Genesis 3:1 ESV

49 Proverbs 23:7 ESV

50 Ibid.

51 Philippians 4:8 ESV

52 Romans 12:2 ESV

53 Chambers, Oswald, *The Complete Works of Oswald Chambers* (Discovery House), 580.

54 Romans 10:17 ESV

55 1 Corinthians 2:16 ESV

56 Exodus 3:2 ESV

57 2 Corinthians 4:7 ESV

58 Romans 11:29 ESV

59 Revelation 3:17 ESV

60 Ezekiel 34:2 ESV

61 Revelation 3:21 ESV

62 Chambers, Oswald, *The Complete Works of Oswald Chambers* (Discovery House), 12.

63 Revelation 3:18 ESV

64 John 3:16 ESV
65 Revelation 22:17 ESV
66 Jonah 2:9 ESV
67 Isaiah 44:14-20 ESV
68 https://www.merriam-webster.com › dictionary › kangaroo court
69 *The World's Best Poetry*, ed. by Bliss Carman, et al. Philadelphia: John D. Morris & Co., 1904; Bartleby.com, 2012.
70 1 Samuel 2:23 ESV
71 https://www.songfacts.com › facts › lynn-anderson › i-never-promised-you-a-rose-garden
72 John 15:18 ESV
73 2 Timothy 3:12 ESV
74 2 Corinthians 4:4 ESV
75 1 John 2:15 ESV
76 John 12:31,32 ESV
77 John 16:33 ESV
78 Proverbs 6:17 ESV
79 Proverbs 27:17 ESV
80 https://www.goodreads.com › quotes › 54835-everyone-is-a-moon-and-has-a-dark-side-which
81 Psalm 39:1-4 ESV
82 Hebrews 12:15 ESV
83 Romans 12:17,18 ESV
84 Matthew 24:30 ESV
85 John Adams to Mercy Otis Warren, April 16, 1776. A. Koch and W. Peden, eds., The Selected Writings of John and John Quincy Adams (Knopf, New York, 1946), p. 57.
86 Genesis 6:5 ESV
87 Will H. Dilg, *The DeKalb Daily Chronicle*, vol. 25, no. 285, November 9, 1925, DeKalb, Illinois
88 Psalm 46:1 ESV
89 Psalm 60:11 ESV
90 Hebrews 13:5 ESV
91 1 Corinthians 13:12 ESV
92 Benge, Janet &Geoff, *C.S. Lewis, Master Storyteller* (YWAM Publishing), 189.
93 Matthew 11:28 ESV
94 Ephesians 5:14 ESV
95 Acts 22:6 ESV
96 Philippians 1:23 ESV
97 https://www.goodreads.com › quotes › 470-it-is-a-far-far-better-thing-that-i-do
98 Benge, Janet &Geoff, *C.S. Lewis, Master Storyteller* (YWAM Publishing), 189.

99 Isaiah 17:12,13 ESV

100 Chambers, Oswald, *The Complete Works of Oswald Chambers* (Discovery House), 303.

101 Daniel 7:3 ESV

102 1 Corinthians 15:3,4 ESV

103 Colossians 1:27 ESV

104 2 Corinthians 5:7 ESV

105 John 15:4 ESV

106 Isaiah 55:1 ERSV

107 Galatians 2:21 ESV

108 Matthew 11:28-30 ESV

109 2 Timothy 1:6 ESV

110 Hebrews 12:28 ESV

111 Lewis, C.S., *The Beloved Works of C.S. Lewis, The Four Loves* (Inspirational Press), 251.

112 Job 5:7 ESV

113 https://www.bobdylan.com › songs › times-they-are-changin

114 1 Kings 19:2 ESV

115 1 Kings 19:9 ESV

116 Matthew 16:18 ESV

117 Mark 8:36 ESV

118 2 Timothy 1:7 ESV

119 Luke 12:32 ESV

120 Psalm 118:11,12 ESV

121 Romans 8:31 ESV

122 Joshua 5:2-9 ESV

123 1 John 5:4 ESV

124 John 16:33 ESV

125 Fischer, Davis Hackett, *Washington's Crossing* (Oxford University Press), 42.

126 2 Timothy 3:1,2 ESV

127 Revelation 2:10 ESV

128 Luke 12:51 ESV

129 Genesis 4:1 ESV

130 Revelation 5:2 ESV

131 Revelation 5:5 ESV

132 Revelation 5:7-14 ESV

133 2 Timothy 3:1 ESV

134 Tozer, A.W., *The Knowledge of the Holy* (Walker and Company), 1,2.

135 Revelation 1:17 ESV

136 Revelation 4:8 ESV

137 Revelation 4:11 ESV

138 Daniel 10:9 ESV

139 Matthew 17:4 ESV

140 Isaiah 6:5 ESV

141 Luke 17:21 ESV

142 1 Corinthians 15:5 ESV

143 Acts 2:36 ESV

144 2 Timothy 1:7 ESV

145 Joshua 10:25 ESV

146 Hopkins, Evan, *The Law of Liberty in the Spiritual Life* (Christian Literature Crusade), 156.

147 Romans 8:31 ESV

148 Luke 19:5 ESV

149 Luke 19:8 ESV

150 Exodus 33:11 ESV

151 Joshua 1:2 ESV

152 1 Corinthians 15:55 ESV

153 Genesis 1:1 ESV

154 Ibid.

155 Hebrews 11:6 ESV

156 https//selfeducatedamerican.com › 2018 › 03 › 20 › isaac-newton-man-of-science-and-faith

157 Psalm 19:1 ESV

158 Daniel 5:1-4 ESV

159 Dan 5:25-28 ESV

160 Galatians 2:20 ESV

161 augustinianspirituality.org › 2022 › 01 › 18 › restless-until-we-rest-in-god-2

162 Jeremiah 29:11 KJV ESV

163 (Hebrews 11:1 ESV

164 Isaiah 45:22 ESV

165 Chambers, Oswald, *The Complete Works of Oswald Chambers* (Discovery House), 604.

166 Romans 8:18 ESV

167 Hummel, Charles, *Tyranny of the Urgent* (InterVarsity Press), 11.

168 Mark 6:5 ESV

169 Ibid.

170 Titus 3:1 ESV

171 Luke 12:10 ESV

172 Lewis, C.S., *Mere Christianity* (HarperCollins Publishers), 52.

173 John 16:8-11 ESV

174 John 16:13 ESV

175 Hebrews 3:15 ESV

176 Matt 19:14 ESV

177 1 Samuel 1:14 ESV

178 Ecclesiastes 2:15,16 ESV

179 Romans 8:24,25 ESV

180 Titus 2:12,13 ESV

181 2Timothy 1:12 ESV

182 Revelation 2:10 ESV

183 Hebrews 13:5 ESV

184 Jeremiah 29:11 ESV

185 https://www.webster-dictionary.org › definition › open secret

186 Luke 2:49 ESV

187 Luke 2:51) ESV

188 2 Timothy 3:15 ESV

189 1 Kings 22:8 ESV

190 1Kings 22:14 ESV

191 1Kings 22:15 ESV

192 1Kings 22:16 ESV

193 1 Kings 22:18 ESV

194 1 Kings 22:19-23 ESV

195 1 Kings 22:23 ESV

196 www.oldsouth.org › truth-forever-scaffold

197 2 Timothy 4:3 ESV

198 2 Thessalonians 2:10-12 KJV

199 Chambers, Oswald, *The Complete Works of Oswald Chambers* (Discovery House), 12.

200 Romans 7:18 ESV

201 Matthew 16:23 ESV

202 Luke 22:31 ESV

203 1 Corinthians 15:5 ESV

204 genius.com › Three-dog-night-one-lyrics

205 1 Kings 17: 13,14 ESV

206 www.christian.org.uk › resource › Athanasius-against-the-world

207 1 Kings 19:18 ESV

208 Psalm 55:22 ESV

209 Ibid. 598.

210 Matthew 16:18 ESV

211 Acts 7:51) ESV

212 Acts 7:56 ESV

213 Acts 7:60 ESV

214 Lewis, C.S., *The Beloved Works of C.S. Lewis, Surprised by Joy* (Inspirational Press), 116.

215 Proverbs 27:17 ESV

216 Job 16:2 ESV

217 2 Samuel 12:1-4 KJV

218 2 Samuel 12:7 ESV

219 Proverbs 27:6 ESV

220 Ibid.

221 Brown,, Daniel James, *Facing the Mountain* (Viking), 352

222 Matthew 10:28 ESV

223 Revelation 20:6 ESV

224 John 19:30 ESV

225 Foxe, John Rev., *Foxe's Book of Martyrs* (Fleming H. Revell Company), 17.

226 Revelation 12:11 ESV

227 Philippians 1:21 ESV

228 John 15:5 ESV

229 James 1:6 ESV

230 James 2:14 ESV

231 Nee, Watchman, *The Normal Christian Life* (Tyndale House Publishers, Inc.), 82,83.

232 Exodus 34:14 ESV

233 Chambers, Oswald, *The Complete Works of Oswald Chambers* (Discovery House), 899

234 Hebrews 11:6 ESV

235 John 3:3 ESV

236 Acts 8:31 ESV

237 Ephesians 2:8,9 ESV

238 Luke 16:28 ESV

239 Isaiah 53:3 ESV

240 Zephaniah 3:17 ESV

241 Tozer, A.W., *The Knowledge of the Holy* (Walker and Company), 185,186.

242 library.timelesstruths.org › music › The Love_of_God

243 Matthew 23:13 ESV

244 John 19:30 ESV

245 Chambers, Oswald, *The Complete Works of Oswald Chambers* (Discovery House), 1045.

Printed in the United States
by Baker & Taylor Publisher Services